The Oneness Guide for Today

"This book is a gentle yet profound reminder that we are all deeply interconnected. Faith Spencer offers tools that empower readers to let go of stress and embrace a life of joy and unity. I couldn't recommend it more."
   —**Marci Shimoff,** #1 *New York Times* best-selling author of *Happy for No Reason* and *Chicken Soup for the Woman's Soul*

"The truth of our existence is that everything is energy and we are all connected, and I'm so glad that Faith Spencer is helping young women realize this so they can see life differently and live more peacefully."
   —**Dr. Sue Morter,** #1 *LA Times* and *USA Today* bestselling author of *The Energy Codes*

"*The Oneness Guide for Today* is a treasure! It guides teens to the truths that will help them live more fulfilling lives: We are all connected, we are never alone, and we can follow our inner knowing to find what's meant for us in life. I can't imagine anything better!"
   —**Suzanne Giesemann,** spiritual teacher and author of *The Awakened Way, Making the Afterlife Connection,* and *Wolf's Message*

"It is rare to see the post-materialist paradigm that is gradually coming in vogue explained suitably for young adult readers. I highly recommend this book."
   —**Amit Goswami,** PhD, co-author with Valentina R. Onisor of *The Return of the Archetypes* and *Quantum Spirituality*

"With compassion and clarity, Faith Spencer illuminates the path to oneness in a way that feels deeply personal and universally relevant. This book is a treasure trove of insights, affirmations, and practices that will uplift and inspire readers of all ages, but especially teens and young adults."
   —**Sherrie Dillard,** medical intuitive, counselor, and author of *I'm Still With You*

"Although *The Oneness Guide for Today* speaks specifically to young women, the clearly written information would be useful to a person of any age seeking to expand their personal growth and ability to live well… I wish I could go back into my insecure teenaged years with this affirming book of guidance in hand! Thank you, Faith, for providing such an empowering head start for young women.

    —**Daeryl Holzer,** author of *A Feather for My Love* and *Opening a Window to the Soul*

"This lovely spiritual guide for young women comes from an author who truly cares about their well-being. It's a book that helps young people open up to the oneness of the world around them while also encouraging them to travel within to explore their own sacred one, or self."

    —**Tanya Carroll Richardson,** author of *Zen Teen* and *Angel Intuition*

"Faith Spencer's book helps young people find a sense of inner peace and happiness that isn't dependent on external circumstances. This is so important! Teens today are struggling, but there is hope, and Spencer's book is one of the sources of hope!"

    —**Kylie Dean,** speaker, Wellbeing Coach, and founder of Purely Happiness (www.purelyhappiness.com.au)

"We are here for a reason, and we all have a soul purpose. Faith Spencer's book encourages young people to tap into the wisdom about their place in the world that is already within them. She also helps them connect with the greater universe to create lives based on a deep sense of guidance. Such a valuable gift to have when you're young!"

    —**Kathy Kwiatkowski,** MS, licensed counselor, LBL hypnotherapist, and author of Stand in Your Brilliance

"Spencer empowers young people to embrace themselves and life in this uplifting guide. The text seamlessly blends contemporary references (Post Malone, TikTok) with timeless wisdom from deep thinkers like the Buddha, effectively bridging the gap between modern teens and ancient philosophies."

    —**Kirkus Reviews**

The Oneness Guide for Today

A BOOK OF INSIGHT FOR YOUNG WOMEN

Faith Spencer

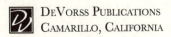
DeVorss Publications
Camarillo, California

The Oneness Guide for Today

Copyright © 2025
by Faith Spencer

All rights reserved. No part of this book may be reproduced,
stored, or transmitted in any form without permission in writing
from the publisher, except by a reviewer who may quote
brief passages for review purposes.

PRINT ISBN: 978-087516-959-0
EBOOK ISBN: 978-087516-960-6

Library of Congress Control Number: 2025931768

This publication is offered with the understanding that
the publisher and author are not giving psychological, medical,
financial, legal, or other professional advice.
If such assistance is needed by the reader, please seek
the services of a licensed professional.

First Printing, 2025
DeVorss & Company, Publisher
P.O. Box 1389
Camarillo CA 93011-1389
www.devorss.com

Printed in the United States of America

Quick Coherence Technique:
HeartMath is a registered trademark of Quantum Intech, Inc.
For all HeartMath trademarks,
go to www.heartmath.com/trademarks.

For Grace

Table of Contents

Introduction ix

Possible Ways to Use This Book xiii

Part One: Understanding Your Oneness 1

Chapter 1 How You Perceive Yourself 3

Chapter 2 How You See the World Around You 17

Chapter 3 Meeting Your Ego 29

Chapter 4 Understanding You're Not Alone 43

Chapter 5 Discovering Your Own Unique Oneness 53

Chapter 6 Feeling Your Oneness 67

Part Two: Discovering Oneness in Our World 75

Chapter 7 Appreciating the World's Different Perspectives . . . 77

Chapter 8 Spiritual Perspectives on Oneness 87

Chapter 9 Scientific Perspectives on Oneness 97

Chapter 10 Oneness Helps Create a More Harmonious World . . 109

Part Three: Putting Your Oneness Into Practice.....115

Chapter 11 Utilizing Oneness to Find Your Purpose 117

Chapter 12 Tuning In to Your Inner Compass 137

Chapter 13 Following Your Intuition 151

Chapter 14 Opening Your Heart to Forgiveness 167

Chapter 15 Making Positive Changes...................185

Chapter 16 Stepping Into Your Destiny............... 211

Chapter 17 Putting It All Together................... 231

Onward 237

Further Reading and Listening 240

FAITH SPENCER

"There is a life-force within your
soul, seek that life.
There is a gem in the mountain
of your body, seek that mine.
O traveler, if you are in search of That
Don't look outside, look inside
yourself and seek That."

—RUMI

Introduction

JUST LIKE YOU, I was once a confused teen, then a struggling young adult. Years later, when my first and only child was born, I thought about the challenges most young people face in this fast-paced and overwhelming world. This inspired me to create a new road map for others to follow, so my daughter wouldn't have to take the same challenging and winding roads I'd taken.

I parented her with empathy and attentiveness, encouraging her to blossom into who she was meant to be. I believe that when children are given respect and unconditional love, they can grow up to become agents of change in a world that sorely needs them.

In considering my child's future path, I asked: Would it not be more empowering for her to be able to answer all the questions she may face when she becomes a teenager? Questions like "Why are people mean sometimes?" or "Why am I so different from others?" or "How do I know my purpose in life?"

I was inspired to write down my thoughts in an encouraging guide, to help her and other young people navigate their unique paths, encouraging life-changing shifts in perspective and helping them become the heroes of their own journeys.

As a certified "Happy for No Reason" trainer, I teach teens and young adults how to embrace who they are and become unconditionally happy. These life-changing techniques help people increase their happiness from the inside out and become less dependent on external situations for their good feelings.

Most young people receive old-school instructions, which include a lot of outdated ideas like "Always be nice" and "Don't rock the boat." Or "Look good above all else" and "Try your best to be popular." These confusing sayings make us think we have to fight for what is ours, because we are alone in the world. In fact, underlying every single one of the instructions listed above is one gigantic misunderstanding: You are a separate person living in a world of separate things, and you have to struggle alone to make things work out for you.

The new discovery I offer in this book is that you are actually connected with everything. Because of this, you don't have to live in a state of stress and struggle. *You are an interconnected being who is one with the Universe.* When you really understand this truth, you can begin to see a new reality that truly feels good.

My hope is that this book will introduce you to many new, practical ways of navigating a more conscious and happy life. It might take a while to explore and implement all the practices presented in this book, and that's okay.

As you use these explorations to update your life road map, you'll begin to navigate life with a different compass—one that leads you to exactly where you're meant to be. You'll feel more purposeful, as if your destiny has always been leading you to be here right now. You'll know you have the power to create your own life on your own terms, while welcoming a lot of help from the Universe along the way.

Are you ready to get started?

Possible Ways to Use This Book

As you explore this book, you may consider not only reading it, but also putting it into practice. The book's guidance and ideas might change how you perceive and live your life—in a great way! Here are just a few ways to make this book work for you:

One and done. Just reading this book one time is great, and doing so certainly will imbue you with much-needed perspectives, new ideas, and positive feelings. The more you are "vibing" on a high note, the more you'll start to find good things around you.

Read as needed. After reading the book, you don't have to put it on a shelf (or let it collect virtual dust in your Kindle library); it can continue to be useful in your life. Anytime you're feeling down or frustrated or like life just isn't going your way, you can pick up the book and open it to the part that you need. Allow it to lift you up and change your perspective. This book can function like a caring friend and counselor who never lets you down and always knows the *real* truth about you. Just being in that friend's presence fills you with more hope and positivity.

Write in it. At the end of each chapter, you'll find exploratory exercises that invite you to reflect on the concepts presented. Additional exercises and audio versions can be found at FaithSpencer.com/explorations. If you find an exercise you like, try doing it daily for a month to give it a chance to have a real effect.

Use the affirmations. You will find an affirmative statement at the beginning of each section that has been provided for you to say to yourself for a period of time. You may even want to tear one or more affirmations out of the book and hang them on your wall. (Yes, I just said that—you are welcome to *wreck this journal!*)

I hope you will refer to this book often, no matter where you are at in your life's journey, and that it will help as you embody a more beautiful, peaceful, vibrant, loving, extra-awesome-special-amazing-wonderful you!

Part One

Understanding Your Oneness

AFFIRMATIONS

I am willing to see the truth about life.

I know my happiness is in my own hands
and my perspective is everything.

I let go of my ego's ideas and allow myself
to flourish as an interconnected being
who is one with the Universe.

FAITH SPENCER

"Learn to see.
Realize that everything
connects to everything else."

—LEONARDO DA VINCI

CHAPTER ONE

How You Perceive Yourself

Y OU ARE AMAZING AND WONDERFUL. That's the truth! You were created to be the way you are, and you're perfect. Let that sink in for a minute.

Now, you may think something like: *What?! This author doesn't know me at all. I'm not perfect. I'm not even close to perfect*! If any thoughts like that are currently swirling around in your mind, you're part of a club that includes pretty much every person on the planet.

These self-doubting feelings are natural and stem from another truth that doesn't sound quite as full of sunshine and rainbows: Life can be pretty hard. As wonderful as the teen and young adult years can be, they can also be a very confusing and disorienting time.

As you've probably noticed, during this time your life can change in dramatic ways. Your body, clothing, friends, and activities have likely started looking different from before. Whereas everything used to seem so simple and easy, the blissful innocence of childhood is fading into the past.

When you were younger, your biggest concerns were probably which flavor of ice cream you wanted or if the weather was good enough to go to the park. Your major decisions back then? Whether you should have a grilled cheese or PB&J. Now, your decisions are more serious, and you might feel the weight of it all on your shoulders.

These days, you may feel you have to constantly compete for top grades, social media likes or followers, potential boyfriends and girlfriends, and accomplishments to put on your college applications or résumé. It can seem like you must be "on stage" all the time and make a steady stream of high-stakes decisions that will affect your future. It can be overwhelming and seem like you are constantly navigating life-altering situations.

You may also encounter negative comments online or from others in your everyday life. People aren't always nice, and your parents can't always protect you from the people around you. Like the band Twenty One Pilots states in their song "Stressed Out," you may sometimes wish you could turn back time to the days when life was so much easier.

Granted, there are many upsides to getting older—getting your driver's license is a fantastic step forward on the path to personal freedom, right? Still, there are undeniable pressures and frustrations you can experience during these years. Just because there are challenges doesn't mean you have to suffer; there's plenty of hope for feeling better than you may be feeling right now.

The reason there's so much hope for improvement is that a lot of the stress you may feel during this time comes from your perceptions. This includes how you perceive yourself and the world around you.

Where Self-Perception Comes From

Even though we might like to think that our self-image is something we came up with ourselves, our self-perception often comes largely from the world around us. Instead of being in charge of our own minds, countless environmental influences shape our ideas about who we are and what we ought to be. For instance, our parents and grandparents constantly weigh in on what they think we should do or be (even offering seemingly benign statements like "be a good student").

At an early age, we start to believe certain descriptions of ourselves. Are you the "good one" in your family or the "troublemaker"? Are you "creative," or are you more "athletic"? Are you "clumsy" or "competent"? Are you "smart" or "school-challenged"? Often, it's someone else who told us we were those things.

We also take note of all the things other people—including our friends, our community, and the greater world—deem important. We see people on TV and the internet living a certain way (Skinny? Check. Famous? Check. Rich? Check, check, check). Over time, we form our opinions on what we "should" achieve.

You might call it the "sponge method" of living life. We absorb other people's ideas about how to live our best lives. Strangely, we absorb these ideas even though we don't know how happy those people we're emulating (like celebrities or influencers) *truly* are.

Whether it's through comparison with others, how others compliment us, or how they admonish or tease us, we form a self-concept. Because of this, we feel a certain way about ourselves based on other people's opinions and decide that whatever verdict has been thrown to us is what we *are* and *have to be*.

We cling to those ideas about ourselves, almost as if our survival is at stake. We push others away if they don't support this self-concept and welcome them if they fit our ideas about ourselves. *(You complimented me on my fashion? Welcome to my "friends club." You don't find my humor funny? You just became invisible to me. You wear goofy-looking glasses? We won't be socializing much. You gave me an F? That's not acceptable and my parents will be in touch with you!)*

It can sometimes feel like we're struggling for our lives, always at war with the world around us, needing things to be "just so" in order to be okay. We must achieve certain grades, a certain appearance, a certain image on social media, this many followers, and a certain level of success in our activities.

Taking Back the Power to Define Yourself

We have to ask ourselves: Are we happy with this situation? As we absorb the world's ideas about ourselves and our lives, does it really make us feel content, peaceful, and right inside? Or do we need to step back and reconsider who we *really* are and what *really* matters?

Instead of continuing to be sponges, we need to

become more self-determined. We need to find a new way to look at ourselves. And while we're at it, we need to learn more about who we *really* are. Are we really our grades? Our appearance? Our social media activity? Our popularity status? Or are we much, much more than that?

As you learn more about oneness, you'll realize some little-known truths about who you are beneath the surface, way down deep inside. You don't have to remain confused about your identity or wonder whether you fit in. You'll discover you are something much more amazing than you realized. You're part of a greater whole, and you're already a complete human being.

By reading this book, you will come to see yourself differently. What's more, you'll realize you are not in this alone; you are merged with everything, living in a state of oneness with everything you need and want. This is an inborn state that never goes away, and it means you are always connected with life.

I know this may sound strange, which is understandable. It's not the way we normally view things. This fact also may come as a big relief, because it means that you don't have to struggle or to try so hard. You can trust in a greater plan and purpose for your life and know that there is a greater Universe always supporting you and accessible to you.

As you change your self-perceptions—including adopting a perception of yourself as an interconnected being in a benevolent Universe—you will feel more peaceful, confident, and self-assured. You'll feel happier deep down inside knowing there are a host of benefits in your life that are practical and real.

Are you ready to transform your entire worldview? Let's do this!

> "Worthiness is not something that is assigned from the outside; it is something that you practice."
>
> —ESTHER HICKS

EXPLORATIONS

Appreciating Ourselves

We all get into the habit of taking ourselves for granted. But we need to get in the habit of seeing ourselves in all our glory. We do a lot of great things! As we focus our attention on what we like about what we're doing, this builds an inner source of self-acceptance.

What are the things you do every day that you could appreciate more? Simple things like taking care of a pet, completing your chores, or helping someone out at school are noteworthy accomplishments!

We think what we are doing is "ordinary," but we could just lie in bed all day every day eating fruit snacks—but we don't! (Or at least not usually...for an entire day...um, do we?)

INSTRUCTIONS

Throughout the day, give yourself some acknowl-edgement for the little things you are succeeding in (especially those things that adhere to your own standards of success, like being kind, being creative, or being there for others).

WRITE IT DOWN

List things here that you appreciate yourself for doing—and which you often take for granted!

ADD TO THIS LIST ANYTIME

1 _____

2 _____

3 _____

4 _____

5 _____

6 _____

7 _____

8 _____

9 _____

10 _____

ALSO TRY THIS:

For one month, each night at bedtime, write down or say to yourself three things you appreciate about yourself that day. You'll start feeling better overall as you offer yourself appreciation and notice what's going well.

Turning Your Thoughts Around

Byron Katie, author of *Loving What Is*, shares a method to free ourselves from negative thoughts so that we can feel more accepting of life exactly as it is. She calls it the "Four Questions" and "The Turnaround."

These questions invite you to explore whether there are other angles from which to view situations and whether you truly know the whole story. You're invited to question your assumptions and find the deeper truth, or bigger reality, that lies beneath them. You'll come to see that you really can free yourself from harmful thought patterns, leaving you free to live more happily. For more about this method, visit TheWork.com.

The following is extracted from Byron Katie's "Judge Your Neighbor Worksheet for Teens and Young Adults" (available for free at TheWork.com). She also has a wonderful app that allows you to do the work right on your phone.

Think of a time when you were really upset with someone. Remember the exact moment when you were most upset with them. Go back to that moment and answer the questions on the next page. Write what you really think.

1. Who made you angry, sad, scared, or disappointed? Why did you feel that way?

2. At that moment, how did you want them to change? What did you want them to do?

3. What should they or shouldn't they have done?

Now pick one of the statements that you wrote above and answer the four questions below. (It might be like, "My BFF shouldn't hang out with other people without me." Or it could be, "My dad doesn't care about me. If he did, he would talk to me more often.") Close your eyes and wait quietly for the answers that come.

1. Is it true? (Yes or No. If No, move to 3.)

2. Are you really sure that it's true? (Yes or No.)

3. How do you feel when you believe that thought? Does this thought make you happy or sad? Where do you feel these feelings in your body?

4. Who would you be without that thought? Close your eyes and see yourself with that person, in that moment, without the thought. What's it like right now without that thought?

Turn the thought around:

What is the exact opposite of that thought? Is the opposite just as true sometimes, in some way?

When you look at that moment, how is that opposite true? Find one way that it's true. What's another example?

THE ONENESS GUIDE FOR TODAY

Turning Your Thoughts Around

Byron Katie, author of *Loving What Is*, shares a method to free ourselves from negative thoughts so that we can feel more accepting of life exactly as it is. She calls it the "Four Questions" and "The Turnaround."

These questions invite you to explore whether there are other angles from which to view situations and whether you truly know the whole story. You're invited to question your assumptions and find the deeper truth, or bigger reality, that lies beneath them. You'll come to see that you really can free yourself from harmful thought patterns, leaving you free to live more happily. For more about this method, visit TheWork.com.

The following is extracted from Byron Katie's "Judge Your Neighbor Worksheet for Teens and Young Adults" (available for free at TheWork.com). She also has a wonderful app that allows you to do the work right on your phone.

Think of a time when you were really upset with someone. Remember the exact moment when you were most upset with them. Go back to that moment and answer the questions on the next page. Write what you really think.

1. Who made you angry, sad, scared, or disappointed? Why did you feel that way?

2. At that moment, how did you want them to change? What did you want them to do?

3. What should they or shouldn't they have done?

Now pick one of the statements that you wrote above and answer the four questions below. (It might be like, "My BFF shouldn't hang out with other people without me." Or it could be, "My dad doesn't care about me. If he did, he would talk to me more often.") Close your eyes and wait quietly for the answers that come.

1. Is it true? (Yes or No. If No, move to 3.)

2. Are you really sure that it's true? (Yes or No.)

3. How do you feel when you believe that thought? Does this thought make you happy or sad? Where do you feel these feelings in your body?

4. Who would you be without that thought? Close your eyes and see yourself with that person, in that moment, without the thought. What's it like right now without that thought?

Turn the thought around:

What is the exact opposite of that thought? Is the opposite just as true sometimes, in some way?

When you look at that moment, how is that opposite true? Find one way that it's true. What's another example?

Can you turn the thought around another way? Try saying "me" or "my" instead of the other person's name. Has that been true sometimes? In what way has it been true?

1 _____
2 _____
3 _____
_____
_____
_____
_____
_____
_____
_____
_____
_____

4 _____
_____
_____
_____
_____
_____
_____
_____
_____

(Used by permission of Byron Katie.)

"When you change the
way you look at things,
the things you look at change."

—MAX PLANCK

CHAPTER TWO

How You See the World Around You

IN THE LAST CHAPTER, we learned that none of us live isolated lives. For better or worse, we interact with and are influenced by the environment that surrounds us. As a result, not only do we see ourselves in certain ways, but we see the external world in fixed ways as well. And sometimes the way we're looking at the world isn't too helpful; in fact, it can be downright depressing. For instance, have you ever thought something like…

Every time I look at social media, I feel like I'm not enough. Other people seem happier, better.

And I'm always looking at social media.

Sometimes I'm left out of things, and I get major FOMO.

I feel this constant pressure to achieve and be perfect in every way.

People say mean things online so freely, and the news is so disturbing.

What is my future going to be like if I'm already this stressed out and unhappy?

If so, you're definitely not alone.

Teens and young adults today are living in a unique time, which offers both its advantages and disadvantages. They are wiser than ever, know more than young people in the past knew, have more of what they need and want than their parents did, and strive harder to be what they think they should be. I mean, look at all the amazingly creative posts on everyone's social media accounts—aren't they making everyone cooler and more awesome? Yet, happiness-wise, they are coming up short. Sadly, research backs this up. Studies show that we aren't getting any happier. As you may have heard—or experienced firsthand—teenagers as a group seem less happy than they've ever been. The 2024 World Happiness Report revealed that, for the first time, people under 30—including teens and young adults—are less happy than all other age groups in the United States.

That report underscored what other studies have been telling us. The Centers for Disease Control and Prevention (CDC) reported that in 2021, 57 percent of high school girls reported having persistent sadness and hopelessness, and a 2019 Pew Research Center survey showed that 7 out of 10 US teens identify anxiety and depression as a major problem in their peers. The same survey found that 36 percent of girls are "extremely anxious every day."

Although young people sometimes fare worse than any other age group, everyone else isn't doing too well either. Gallup research shows that Americans' stress and worry levels reached a new height in 2018. In 2019, overall happiness was reported at a lower level than in the past 71 years. And in 2024, the United States dropped out of the top 20 happiest countries for the first time in the history of the World Happiness Report, because people of all ages reported decreased levels of happiness.

What does all of that mean? The good news is, it means that if you're feeling a little shaky or on unsteady ground, you're like most other young people your age. We're all struggling on some level. Social media and smartphones make us feel a little high-strung, and instant access to depressing news isn't always a blessing. And when we bury ourselves in social media, it prevents us from dealing with what's really going on in our lives and how we're really feeling.

You see, as we touched on a bit in the last chapter, the culprit that's causing our unhappiness (in most cases) is right there between our ears. The mind—full of the ideas it's absorbed from the world—tells us half-truths and even straight-up lies.

In fact, our brains babble a bunch of nonsense to us all day long, year in and year out.

However, this chatter is often so far beneath the surface that we don't even realize it's going on. Still, you might recognize it as sounding a little bit like this:

I must *get perfect grades and earn awards—my future depends on it!*

I have to *look good in all of my social media posts.*
My body needs *to look like celebrities' and influencers' bodies.*
I can't *do the things I love because there's no time.*
I must *try to be safe from a world that's so scary.*
No one *can know how I really feel; I've got to act cool.*

Our minds spew out lies like this continuously, causing us so much pressure and stress. Before we know it, we're living in a pressure cooker. We're never happy with the current moment—it always needs to be different and better.

When we live like this, it's stressful. Instead of uniting us with others in a happy utopia where we all live peacefully, this type of mindset can be self-focused and isolating: It's *me* against the *rest of the world*, vying to be number one, to be in the lead, and to snag whatever good stuff is out there. (Or at least to try to keep up with those we believe are ahead of us.)

What's even worse is that social media has given our minds lots more ammunition for perpetuating these lies. We see a fake (or, at the very least, a greatly enhanced) version of people's worlds, and we feel inferior to those perfect-looking pictures. This spikes our anxiety and leads to depression.

Selecting Our Perceptions

There's a way out of this dilemma, though. We can be more selective in what we focus on, and we can be more intentional about how we perceive the world. After all, we have more of a choice in how we see things than we may realize.

Psychologist Shawn Achor explains in his book, *Before Happiness*, that studies have shown people can be exposed to 11 million pieces of information every second, but our brains can only process 40 bits of information per second. At any given moment, it's like we are sitting at a beautiful crystal blue lake and only noticing one tiny gray rock. Instead of seeing the whole beautiful scene, we only see a miniscule piece of it. Then we form our opinion of the lake based on that one rock!

According to Achor, "[. . .] every minute of every day, you are merely picking and choosing from the 11 million pieces your senses are receiving." What's more, even two people in the exact same situation will have "two completely different perceptions of the world that are both *equally* true."

Well, that explains a lot of situations, doesn't it? At times, haven't you and your friends remembered the exact same situation or conversation completely differently?

In a sense, we are always perceiving only a tiny slice of reality—a skewed, distorted, self-chosen version. That means we have the power to make our reality a better one by widening our view. How do we do this? According to Achor, we need to realize that multiple realities exist. (You know, like the multiverse!) Then, we can try to enhance our ability to perceive a greater number of ideas and solutions. We can open our minds to the possibilities and viewpoints that we aren't aware of at this current moment.

We always have a choice in how to respond to circumstances, even if it takes a while to pick ourselves up, dust ourselves off, and commit to finding a new perspective. Popular spiritual teacher Matt Kahn reminds us, "It's not the things that happen to me that define how I feel, but the way I choose to see it."

We may not like certain things, but when we realize we have permission to live free of external "shoulds," ideas of "normal," comparisons with others, and other programming we've accepted from the world, we can realize that all is well. We are learning, growing, and changing at our pace, on our own unique paths.

Another popular author, Eckhart Tolle, also insists that we have the power to be happier by purposely viewing situations differently. He says that "Ninety percent of human unhappiness arises not because of situations around you, but because of what your mind is saying about situations in your life."

Ninety percent? Wow! This means that instead of always striving to change our circumstances, we can change our minds. Before we can do that though, we need to talk about a perpetrator that's in our midst, narrowing our focus and causing us to see things in unnecessarily stressful ways. You'll meet that little troublemaker in the next chapter.

> "The world's handbook for living is like an ineffective diet. It's not helpful. It doesn't take us where we need to go."
>
> —SADIE ROBERTSON

EXPLORATIONS

My True Values

We are all products of our environment. However, it's a good idea to disentangle ourselves from environmental influences and develop a sense of who we truly are. This exercise helps you identify what you believe in and value.

INSTRUCTIONS

For this exercise, you will make two lists. Write the heading "My Culture's Values," and make a list of what you observe to be the general goals, aims, and ideals of your culture or family.

What seems to be important? What dominant messages do you receive from your surroundings? It might be especially helpful to write down the messages that have influenced you or caused you stress.

When you're done with that, start writing a new list under the heading "My Values." See if you can identify things that are important to you that differ from what society or your family prescribes.

Your list might be the exact opposite of what is important to society or your family, or it might only be slightly different. You also might realize that some of the positive messages you've received from society (such as, say, valuing family) are also authentic values to you. As you reflect on these two lists, write down what you notice below.

_____
_____
_____
_____
_____

Find the Silver Lining

Sometimes it's hard to accept our current life circumstances. Things aren't always going how we wish they were. For this exercise, try to pull back and look at your life from a larger perspective.

Give yourself a few minutes to sit in a quiet space. Take a few deep breaths and get comfortable. Try to see yourself in your life as if you're watching a movie. Take yourself out of it—maybe put yourself up in the clouds—and just watch it all happening from afar. Notice the dilemmas that are going on with this main character (you). Write them down if you wish.

WRITE IT DOWN

Here is what's going on with this character (me):

_____
_____
_____
_____
_____
_____

Now imagine that you can continue to view your life from this higher vantage point, this broader perspective. What would you say to yourself about the things going on in your life? Let the words come out automatically. Don't think about it; just receive what's there. What is the way to work with this problem, to arrive at a new place with it?

WRITE IT DOWN

This is what this character should do:

_____
_____
_____
_____
_____
_____
_____

"The Ego, however, is not who you really are. The ego is your self-image; it is your social mask; it is the role you are playing. Your social mask thrives on approval. It wants control, and it is sustained by power, because it lives in fear."

—DEEPAK CHOPRA, MD

CHAPTER THREE

Meeting Your Ego

AH YES, THE EGO. Maybe you've heard of it. Many people think the word "ego" refers to someone who seems totally self-obsessed and "full of themselves." "They have a lot of ego," we might say. Actually, that is *part* of what the term ego means, but it's not the entire story. The ego is actually much more insidious (meaning, it creeps into our lives everywhere), wrangling our minds into believing falsehoods in the most unnoticeable, stealthy, and mischievous little manner.

The ego is the part of us that is all about *me*, and it tends to view life in simplistic, neat, black-and-white categories. According to the ego, *I'm here* and everything and everyone else is *way out there*. Everything has a label with a judgment value attached. Everything is either good or bad, right or wrong.

Our egos tend to be fear-based. They tell us things like, "If you don't look good (or aren't successful at a certain thing), it will be *horrible!*" They pretty much lie to us about what's important: namely, our separate selves and everything our small selves might want, such as recognition, approval, money, material values, and power. When we believe the ego, we view life through a lens of "Me, Me, Me."

Our inner conversation goes: *If only I can get all the things I want, then everything will be fine, I will be safe and no longer afraid (of rejection, loss, or failure).* The ego encourages a relentless pursuit of *more* external circumstances that we think will make us happy, but which ultimately won't quite do it. (And the effort itself is exhausting!)

Of course, it's not *only* our own egos saying these things—it's also our *family's* egos saying these things to us, our *friends'* ego selves echoing these ideas, and our *society's* collective egomania, telling us lies about what's important. But listening to the ego isn't helping us get what we want—*if* what we want to be is happy. (And let's face it, everyone wants that!)

Michael Alan Singer explains this in his book *The Untethered Soul*: "The fact is, external changes are not going to solve your problem because they don't address the root of your problem. The root problem is that you don't feel whole and complete within yourself. If you don't identify the root properly, you will seek someone or something to cover it up. You will hide behind finances, people, fame, and adoration." Ouch.

But we're not alone. It's what most of us have been doing—or at least *wanting* to do. It's quite natural. We all want to be adored and to find a sense of security in the world through *something, anything*. However, when we seek those types of solutions, they deliver short-term boosts to our self-worth and a surge of a feel-good brain chemical, dopamine. Unfortunately, we soon come down from our "high" and need another quick boost.

We believed these things provided the answers, but they never did—at least not in the long run. In the book *The Extraordinary Gift of Being Ordinary*, Dr. Ronald D. Siegel explains, "[…] researchers show that people who seek external rewards such as fame, power, wealth, and beauty in pursuit of popularity *have more anxiety, depression, and discontent*—long-term pain."

Chasing The Ego's Perfection

Another reason that following the ego's guidance never makes us happy—or at least not permanently—is that nothing is ever "perfect" for long; conditions are always subject to change. When we base our happiness on things outside of us, it's a losing game, because the truth is, we can't always control things.

Eventually, someone doesn't want to be our friend anymore, we aren't elected class officer, our crush doesn't notice us, our love interest breaks up with us, we get fired from our job (or we can't get the kind we want), we become ill, we look silly on someone's social media feed, we lose an important person or animal, or we may even face dramatic circumstances like becoming homeless.

No matter what befalls us and how we judge those things, underneath it all is the truth which can set us free: In spite of our efforts to distinguish ourselves in this world, we are *not really separate*. We are "one" with everything. Because we've completely forgotten that we are unified and part of a larger whole, we tend to suffer from afflictions like stress, emptiness, loneliness, and longing.

I'm pretty sure I just heard your ego say, "What the heck is this person talking about?! That is just plain bonkers! Just go get back on TikTok! Everything will be just fine, trust me!"

The part of each of us that *knows* this is true—and even important—is the spirit, soul, or deeper essence of ourselves. Somewhere inside, we know that oneness is the truth and that forgetting this truth is a wee bit of a problem.

Little babies know we are all one big, interconnected ball of love, without boundaries and without right and wrong. In fact, until about six months of age, babies *literally* don't know they are separate from their parents. In their perception, everything is more fused together.

In the process of growing up and being in the world, we forget we are all unified together. We "mature" and get more intelligent, and in doing so, we get—basically—dumber about life.

Now, as full-grown (or at least half-grown, or… three-quarters-grown?) humans, on some deep level, we feel we're all islands who operate in a little pocket of "me" apart from all the other "yous."

It *looks* like we are separate. Yet, beneath this illusion that we see in front of us, we are *actually* more like billions of waves in one cohesive, vast sea. This sea connects us in a fundamental way, and we *all* make ripple effects and receive ripple effects constantly. It's kind of amazing to consider this, and it can totally change the way we see the world and live in it.

Finding Peace with Your Ego

Researchers who have analyzed the brains of meditating Buddhist monks and secular individuals during meditation have found that the part of the brain that distinguishes between "me" and "other" (the parietal lobe) quiets down during a meditative state of oneness. When this area is quiet, there is an increased sense of interconnectivity and belonging. No wonder Buddha statues look so happy! Being in touch with oneness feels good.

We need to operate from this new unified perspective and live according to *that* reality if we want to be truly happy—*not* the ego's false reality, which tells us we are separate from everything and that things should always be different and better. (You'll learn how to live from a state of oneness in later chapters.)

When we're in this state, it causes the ego to recede. As explained by neuropsychologist Rick Hanson, author of *Hardwiring Happiness* and *Buddha's Brain*, "The ego subsides when we gain more of a sense of mattering, of receiving belonging."

This just might be what is meant by the expression in the Bible, "The Kingdom of God is within you." Other spiritual teachers describe this center of oneness, including Ernest Holmes, in his book *Living the Science of Mind:* "Peace is at the center of your own soul; It is the very Being of your being. This Peace which is at the center of your being has never been disturbed. It has never been afraid. It never desired to harm anyone; therefore it has never been hurt. How, then, shall you use this great gift which nestles at the very center of your being?"

You have a great gift inside. When you know this place within you, you realize you don't need external factors to be any certain way. You just need to be aware of a deeper truth. And you know what that truth is by now: the truth of oneness. This truth will become clearer and more useful to you as you continue delving into this book.

"Remember that your perception of the world is a reflection of your state of consciousness. You are not separate from it, and there is no objective world out there. Every moment, your consciousness creates the world that you inhabit."

—ECKHART TOLLE

EXPLORATIONS

Accessing Oneness

Put everything down, let everything go, and just be with yourself in silence. Notice your breath. Observe your body's sensations. Notice your thoughts. Take a deep breath in and let it out. Close your eyes if you wish.

Picture yourself surrounded by a bright-white, brilliant light and so much love. This light can feel warm, light, bright, soft, and comforting, like a soft bubble encasing you. Feel yourself connected to something greater, something beyond you that is all-encompassing. Allow yourself to be enfolded in the love and protection that comes from a greater source.

If desired, you can picture yourself connected to a beam of bright light that comes in from above your head and goes all the way down to the base of your spine. This light connects you to the highest point in the Universe or to a realm full of light and love and guidance.

Next, picture yourself rooted to the Earth. You can picture a beam of light, rope, or roots going down from the base of your spine (or your feet, if they are touching the ground) to the center of the Earth. Feel that you're connecting to the Earth's inner core and feel the comforting and calming energy emanating from our beautiful Mother Earth.

Notice you're still connected to the light, while also being rooted to the Earth. Allow yourself to enjoy this peaceful feeling of connection with the Earth, connection with the greater field that binds us all, and unity with everything that exists. Take a breath and feel yourself opening up and becoming a part of everything you can see around you.

Say to yourself, "I am connected with everything." Really take it in. Does it make you feel calmer? Less worried? More okay inside? You might feel a warmth inside or less constriction and tension in your chest. You might notice that your breathing slows down. If you don't notice anything the first time, that's okay too.

When you're ready, end this meditation. Try to take this feeling with you as you go about your day.

Boundaries Blurring

This meditation is a quick way to cultivate a feeling of inner well-being and a sense of being united with everything.

Find a comfortable spot to sit where you can be relaxed. Gently close your eyes if you wish. Bring awareness to your body as it breathes, your chest rising and falling with each breath.

Let yourself feel safe. Let go of any sense of needing to defend yourself from anything or anyone.

Find a sense of just being content with everything as it is. Allow any sense of "I must get this for myself" or "I need to have certain things" to just fall away, fading from your experience.

Also, take a moment to help yourself feel sufficiently connected. Rest in a sense of being loved and loving. Notice that as you do this, any sense of needing to cling to others or to get things from others is falling away. Rest with this sense of satisfaction for a moment or two.

Entertain the thought that there is no pressure to separate yourself from the world to get what you need. You're easing into a growing tranquility, spreading in your body and mind. No strain or struggle is needed.

You are present and receptive to everything. So much

is coming to you peacefully, flowing through you. Each breath is naturally flowing in and naturally flowing out.

The edges of each breath are softening. The edges between the air outside you and the air inside you are also softening. Boundaries are blurring between the inner and the outer. There is a sense of stillness deep inside.

You can broaden your awareness to include a larger perspective that includes this body, room, building, this land, and this community. Have a sense of your body on the Earth, within the solar system, and as part of the vastness of space. View everything as part of a larger whole.

This moment is a local ripple in everything. You are part of everything. You can still function as an individual, while continuing to feel opened into everything.

When you're ready, gently open your eyes. Notice how you feel.

(From "Boundaries Blurring Meditation," Rick Hanson, PhD, Neurodharma Program, RickHanson.com.)

"In order to find yourself, who you really are, you got to be with yourself. You got to hang out with yourself."

—POST MALONE

CHAPTER FOUR

Understanding You're Not Alone

WHAT DID THE BUDDHIST MONK SAY to the hot dog vendor? "Please, make me one with everything." You may or may not love hot dogs with *everything* (after all, that many toppings might overwhelm your taste buds), but being one with everything has a long history of making people feel good. Although it's a radical departure from our usual mindset, oneness isn't a new idea; it's been around for ages. Reggae music legend Bob Marley even sang about oneness in his 1970s song, "One Love, One Heart."

Many famous poets and writers have recognized the reality of oneness. Ralph Waldo Emerson, arguably one of the most famous American writers who's ever lived, penned these profound lines: "We live in succession, in division, in parts, in particles. Meantime within man is the soul of the whole; the wise silence; the universal beauty, to which every other part and particle is equally related, the eternal One."

The poet Rumi expressed a sense of unity with everything way back in the 13th century: "Love said to me, there is nothing that is not me."

These sentiments give the sense that it's all going to be okay. We're not alone; we're fundamentally united with everything, and life is good. Because we are one with everything, we are never alone. But… sometimes it sure feels like we're alone.

Loneliness in the World

The world has been going through a few challenges in recent years. Being a teen can be stressful enough without having to deal with added worries about uber-contagious viruses, climate change, wars, and other pressing world issues. You might have gone through losses during these times, and even temporary losses can have lingering effects.

Even if you're striving your hardest to be positive, the world can impose fearful thoughts on you via the news, world events, social media, and relationship woes. Sometimes it's just all a little too much. It can seem like you're the only one struggling to deal with everything coming at you. You figure you just need to try to "get it together." But you're not alone. No matter how great their pictures look, lots of people out there are secretly feeling the exact same way.

If you feel totally alone, remember that you are actually *never* alone; you are essential to life. You may not be able to control whether or not you are alone right now, but the loneliness you feel, believe it or not, is an opportunity. It's a chance to discover yourself in a whole new way.

When you're feeling isolated, it can be a chance to dig deeper and become more centered, to become clearer about your life, and to fall more in love with yourself. It's a chance to find your own truth, your own beauty, your own wisdom, and the love inside of you that has always been there. It's a chance to get in touch with the beautiful wisdom of the Universe. You just need to learn how.

Alone but Not Lonely

You may have heard about studies that link the feeling of loneliness to mental and physical health problems. That connection may have truth to it, but there's a catch. You can be surrounded by friends or family and still feel lonely, or you can be a monk or nun meditating alone and be filled with a sense of connectedness. Jason Prall, creator of The Human Longevity Project, explains a sense of connection can come from simply tuning in to yourself, to life, to nature, to pets, or to one or two other people: "[Loneliness is] really all about perception."

Using a variety of the exercises in this book, you can perceive yourself and life differently. You can begin to feel more connected to yourself, to life, and to everything. This is true even if nothing on the outside changes. Nothing can taint this underlying wholeness that we all share. Nothing can tarnish the unique and important role we all play in helping humanity to express this total perfection.

Connecting to Our Source

What exactly is this place of wholeness inside? Why do we have the capacity to connect with this place? And why do we normally not feel it? This sense of oneness comes from our connection with an invisible *creative source* that runs through the Universe. This underlying source of love, information, and intelligence is here to support us and is available to us all the time. The only problem is, we rarely realize it.

When we connect with the deeper reality beneath the physical world, we access the pure potential that creates and drives the Universe. This gives us a sense of belonging and a dose of true power. Knowing and feeling this connection is a key to overcoming the problems we face.

This may sound a bit "spiritual" (or straight-up weird) to you. However, you don't have to be particularly religious or spiritually inclined to believe that this source exists. Science also points to the conclusion that there is an underlying creative energy that pervades the Universe. This invisible source of energy, information, and creativity has been called by a variety of names. In religious traditions, it's called God, the Holy Spirit, Allah, Jehovah, Yahweh, Shiva, and much more.

In science, it is called "the unified field," "the matrix," or, in physicist David Bohm's words, "the implicate order." Some people call it the Vortex, Source, Spirit, or Universe. In yoga or ancient healing techniques, this underlying energy can be called ki, chi, qi, or prana.

Ultimately, it's the force of love and oneness we all share, which ties things together in an intricate web of connection. When we tap into this source, we tap into the healing power of love that encompasses everything. And we access the truth about ourselves: We are made of this universal energy.

Whether or not you experience a sense of oneness (which surely you will as you begin to look for it and practice these techniques), what matters—in terms of this book, at least—is that you buy into it, at least to some extent.

Why? Because, for one thing, life is simply better when you believe you are unified with everything and with a creative source. What's more, a belief in oneness will help you understand how the techniques in this book work, including manifestation or co-creation practices, intuitive listening, and forgiveness techniques you'll learn in Part 3. The techniques in this book are effective because of this premise:

If everything is connected, then everything influences everything, and we have the power to influence our well-being and shape our world.

"One day when I was sitting quiet, it came to me: that feeling of being part of everything, not separate at all."

—ALICE WALKER

EXPLORATIONS

Mindful Belly Breathing

Often when we crave things in the outside world, we are really craving our own attention and love. You can fill that void by giving yourself a few minutes of focused attention.

BREATHE IN

Sit or lie down and take some deep belly breaths. Breathe in to the count of four and out to the count of four. Watch the air fill up your chest and belly as it rises, then watch it deflate like releasing air from a balloon. You might try breathing in through your nose and then breathing out through your mouth.

NOTICE YOUR FEELINGS

As you breathe, notice what you feel in your body. Is there an area where you feel sensations of some kind? Tightness, tingling, pain, or warmth? Put your attention there. If it feels right, you could also put your hands there and cradle that part of your body.

SEND LOVE TO YOURSELF

Send love and comfort to that part of your body. Let any emotions arise and keep breathing while they flow out or simply dissipate. Stay with this for 5 to 10 minutes or longer.

"Honor and respect yourself and all of the dreams you were born with. These aren't yours accidentally but are gifts from your higher self. They're part of the very reason you chose to be alive now— to make them come true."

—MIKE DOOLEY

CHAPTER FIVE

Discovering Your Own Unique Oneness

NOW COMES THE PARADOX. You've learned that we are all one. And yet, the truth is, we all do exist as separate people. Right?

You're not just a pile of shifting sand, ready to fall through someone's fingers into nothingness; you're a specific person. This seems rather obvious, because you have straight blonde hair and your friend has curly brown hair. You play piano and your friend plays hockey. You're more humorous and your friend is more uptight and serious. You like your vegetables and your friend lives on soda and candy. (Fortunately, you both like the same Netflix series, so it's all good! Plus, you're not *that* averse to candy, I bet…)

But the fact remains that we're not all the same.

You are a certain person with a name, height, weight, and physical address where you live. You have a self that matters. You have your own thoughts, feelings, and desires that matter, created as a purposeful expression of life with your own special place in the vast scheme of things.

So, if everyone is different, how can we find oneness with the Universe? Do we merge with the Universe, or do we express our uniqueness? It's simple, we do both. You are the entire ocean and you are an individual wave in the ocean.

This sentiment is echoed by Suzanne Giesemann, author of *Wolf's Message*, an intuitive's amazing story of interconnectedness: "You are the whole web [of interconnection] *and* the individual expression of it."

You are the uniqueness that you bring to the world as that individual expression. You can be a sweet little wave, just doing your own thing, while being aware of your connection with the ocean. Your unique truth is about who you are and why you're here. As you learn to better appreciate and express yourself, you'll see how important you are to the underlying flow of life and where you belong.

And even though you've been yourself for your

whole life, I bet sometimes you still wonder: *Who am I?*

This question is an important one: Who is this little individual wave that you are? What makes it flow and roll around in the ocean with harmony and bliss?

Most of us explain who we are with specific qualifiers: This is my name, I'm this age, I came from a certain family; I am really good at certain things, like playing harmonica and acting super goofy to make people laugh.

But is any of that who you are?

And beyond *who* you are—*why* are you? Are you here for a reason? Is it just to get good grades and, along the way, have some good times and take some killer selfies?

We all want that "aha" moment in life when it feels like we are standing at the top of an enormous mountain and looking down with complete and total understanding of the entire world. In an instant, we see our lives as if through a crystal ball, and suddenly we smack ourselves on the forehead, exclaiming, "Duh! I get it now! Why didn't I always know what my life was all about? It's so totally and completely obvious!"

This is a valid desire, because we are purposely designed to have a special place in the world as ourselves, not as a mixture of everyone else. We were created to be something that's never existed before and never will exist again. But what exactly is that?

In order to find those answers, we need to first understand why we matter and how we fit into the wholeness of life.

The Beauty of Being Different

You've got to admit, you probably don't always notice your oneness with everything. Most likely, you don't feel like you are connected. Instead, you look around and think, *I am* nothing *like that person—we are from different planets entirely! Either I don't belong, or* they *don't belong.*

Although seemingly different, we are all unique manifestations of oneness. It's like the Universe is this big, beautiful wholeness that we are all a portion of. You can think of humanity like a delicious casserole. In this casserole, the garlic and salt are as important as the noodles and cheese. In fact, it wouldn't be a great tasting casserole without each ingredient.

If the pasta wasn't there, it wouldn't be a casserole. (Do you sometimes feel a little like just a bunch of floppy noodles? Yet you somehow are holding everything and everyone together?) Without the cheese, it wouldn't be as comforting and creamy. (We all know someone who has that comforting smoothness to them—and, yes, they might be a little bit "cheesy"!) And if the pepper wasn't there, it wouldn't be as exciting. (I bet you can think of someone who's a little zingy and pepper-y! Or maybe that's you!)

There is a flip side to everything. You might think, "I'm so quiet." But the hidden gem in that may be that you're observant, making you a good writer, or actress, or even a compassionate and astute counselor.

Maybe you think, "I'm so loud and rambunctious. I'm 'too much' for people." But those traits make you the perfect one to speak up and raise awareness about important things, or to help others in crisis situations, or to shine brightly as an entertainer. Maybe you make people laugh, and laughter is healing for everyone. (It's true; frequent laughter can literally heal your body, so it's no small thing.)

Maybe something bad happened to you, which tempts you to feel sorry for yourself. But that unfortunate thing may be the catalyst that allows you to be helpful to so many others with similar problems, which the world has needed all along. Whatever you're dealing with that makes you feel "different," know that it's not a mistake. You're learning, growing, and shining a unique light on the world, which brightens everything up.

We're not meant to be alike or uniform, like factory-made toys. Instead, it's like the Universe wants there to be every different type of person. Wholeness is the goal. All the colors, shapes, personalities, and temperaments among us are meant to be there as unique creations that, when combined, comprise the complete wholeness of all. You fit into this. You are a part of the beautiful design that has been created intentionally. The world needs you and what you can offer to others.

The True Self

As a part of oneness, we are meant to be our most *true* selves (and not try to be more like someone else), to help each other be happy, and to keep creating more and more love in the world. We're intended to grow up and become a world of people who love unconditionally, without restrictions, without division.

But what if we seem to be "naturally" angry or selfish? I'm not saying to go ahead and be that way. We aren't just supposed to express the hurtful parts of ourselves or cause harm to others and say, "That's just me." We are here to grow in many ways and learn how to be more peaceful and to have a positive influence. Sometimes we can act in ways that are critical, selfish, or outright mean. This happens because we don't feel quite right within ourselves. Something is off, unsettled, or downright depressing within us. When this happens, we can always get support to find our way back to feeling good, kind, and happy. When others act those ways, they need to do the same. Maybe deep down we're sad, hurt, or scared. Maybe we're having hormonal changes that are causing our emotions to run wild. Still, we can always find ways to rebalance ourselves.

Embracing Your Essential Essence

If you're still not convinced that you belong here just as much as everyone else, *exactly* as you are, then ask yourself this: What makes your friends and the people in your life enjoyable? Think about your friends and even relatives you enjoy being with. Do you like them because they look a certain way, or because they get good grades, or wear cool clothes, have a good job, have perfect bodies, or have a steady boyfriend/girlfriend? Most likely, you couldn't care less about those things—you would want to be around them no matter what!

I mean, don't get me wrong, stylish friends and cousins are perfectly wonderful, but not essential.

Why? It's because what we enjoy about someone is not their hairstyle, their clothing, or their weight on a scale; it's their *essence*. It sounds strange, but it's true: You're drawn to the energy that radiates from their personality, their unique way of expressing themselves, and the unique light they shine on the world and upon you.

In some ways, it's not our "specialness" that makes us appealing to others, but our beautiful ordinariness—the way others can see themselves in us when we are just being authentically ourselves.

It's sometimes hard to see it this way, but this is true for all of us. We aren't here to meet requirements; we're here to be *exactly who we are*. Goofy, silly, sometimes clueless, sometimes draped in ill-fitting clothing, sometimes quiet, sometimes outrageous, and always just plain *us*.

Redefining Greatness

There is something great within each of us, and we are all made for greatness. But the truth is, we *really* need to redefine greatness. Greatness isn't about being a financially successful person or famous. You're not "finally someone" when your picture is plastered all over the internet. Greatness is about the small things that make a difference. It's about making tiny positive ripple effects. For example:

Greatness is taking care of small creatures.

Greatness is listening with a compassionate ear.

Greatness is saying something nice when we could have stayed silent.

Greatness is watering a flower.

Greatness is singing a pretty song.

Greatness is petting an animal.

Greatness is loving yourself even when you let yourself or others down.

Greatness is giving what you have to others, when that feels good to you.

Greatness is just being you and doing what you love to do and what feels totally right to you.

Greatness is filling the world with a bit more love and light, just by doing something small like helping your neighbor, giving your mom a hug, or telling your friend you like them.

In the words of author Suzanne Giesemann, "You can do a great thing just by showing someone that they're loved." Yes, it is that simple. We are all miracle workers just by being here. We help others around us in so many ways that we don't even realize, as unique and intentional expressions of the oneness of the Universe. And that is true about you even if:

You don't always feel happy.

You sometimes feel out of place.

You don't feel like you meet certain requirements to be popular or attractive or "perfect."

You've done bad things.

You don't feel like you're motivated to do anything special.

What's way more important than any of this is whether you are expressing your true self and whether you make a positive difference in even *one* life. We need to see ourselves as the Universe does—as an amazing piece of the puzzle, without which the whole thing wouldn't even work.

"Don't you ever let a soul in the world tell you that you can't be exactly who you are."

—LADY GAGA

EXPLORATIONS

Things About Me

We are all unique. What are the unique things about you that other people have noticed? Write them down. (Even if it's embarrassing. No one else has to see this!):

Make a list of the unique things about you that other people haven't noticed, but that you've noticed about yourself and think are important. (Again, no one else has to see this, and no one has to even agree! How freeing is that? This is between you and your inner self or the Universe.)

_____
_____
_____
_____
_____
_____
_____
_____
_____

Supporting Yourself Like a Friend

We are often harder on ourselves than we are on our friends. This exercise helps us apply the same generosity to ourselves that we give to friends. A study showed that saying those affirmations (that you would say to a friend) in front of a mirror promoted a positive feeling of being soothed, as well as greater heart variability, which is a marker of heart health.

FACING A PROBLEM

Think of something that upsets you about yourself or your life right now. What's bothering you lately? Write those things down.

_____
_____
_____
_____
_____
_____
_____
_____

UNDERLYING MESSAGES

What negative things are you saying to yourself about these situations? Are you saying you're not okay or acceptable because of it? Are you judging yourself? Are you directing any frustration or pity your own way? Tune in to why the underlying messages/judgments upset you and write the reasons here.

_____
_____
_____
_____

HELPING YOURSELF

Now imagine that a friend is going through the same situation. What helpful words would you say to your friend about this? Write down at least four sincere statements you might say to make your friend feel better.

_____
_____
_____
_____

For the next week, look in the mirror with your hand over your heart and say those statements to yourself. Notice whether this improves how you feel, even slightly.

"A person is at their absolute best when they get beyond themselves."

—JOE DISPENZA

CHAPTER SIX

Feeling Your Oneness

You might feel a sense of oneness when first waking up in the morning, when you're not quite "in the world" yet. In that hazy state, you're halfway somewhere else, but you notice a fresh optimism and sense of renewal.

You may suddenly be in touch with oneness when you feel an inner glow after hanging out with friends. You may notice it when you stare up at the stars at night. It may come over you when the TV goes off, your phone is dead, and no one is talking. You feel that sense of space, of openness, of something greater beyond this moment that just might be there. It's a feeling that there is something magical surrounding you—something in the air, in the atmosphere, that provides light and ease to your life.

We can all catch glimpses of oneness in our everyday lives, but we need to stay alert for these moments or else we'll miss them. These feelings of interconnectedness can happen spontaneously, through activities such as being out in nature, making or appreciating art or music, or connecting deeply and honestly with another person. They can happen from sitting silently and simply letting go of our attachment to anything—just being in the moment.

We can also invite and welcome a state of unity in more intentional ways, often through meditative-like practices. Some of these practices include yoga, qigong, Tai Chi, meditation, chanting, prayer, and a variety of different breathing or meditative techniques. But don't worry, you don't have to go looking for instructions or classes (although, you certainly can!).

Finding Peace Over the Horizon

As you find ways to feel more unified with everything around you, you'll start to chip away at the false idea that you're isolated and apart from the greater world. Many great minds have tried to explain this sense of connection, including Albert Einstein, who said, "A human being is part of the whole, called by us 'universe,' a part limited in time and space. He experiences himself, his thoughts and feelings as something separate from the rest—a kind of optical delusion of his consciousness."

But how do we break free from this "optical delusion" of separation? One way is through practices and exercises that bring us into a state of oneness.

A super simple way to activate a sense of oneness is to shift your focus. That's all. Does it sound easy? It is! Shifting your vision to a wide-angle view can activate a sense of oneness. When you see the whole picture, it somehow calms you down.

You may not think you've ever experienced a calm feeling while gazing outward, but you probably have. For instance, have you ever noticed that it feels good to gaze out at the horizon? Have you ever stared up at the clouds and felt a total sense of well-being? This is what can happen when you broaden your gaze. It activates an expanded sense of oneness.

What causes this? Brain scientists have found that staring out into the distance engages the calming parts, called the allocentric networks, on the sides of the brain. When we view things that are nearby, we engage the "busy" and "micromanaging" parts that are more down the center of our brains, and we feel more of a sense of ego.

Conversely, when we experience a landscape or sky out in the distance, we see things more as a "whole" and our ego recedes. Some people think the reason this occurs is that this type of focusing activates a switch in a part of the brain called the thalamus that is involved in the release of a neurotransmitter called GABA, which is calming.

Whenever you can view the horizon or look up at the clouds, this not only feels good, but it actually has a positive physical effect on your brain and improves your ability to cope with life's stressors.

The Many Experiences of Oneness

Just like staring out at a landscape, which we all do naturally, feeling connected with everything can be simple. It doesn't have to feel like an inner earthquake, forever altering your world. It can simply be a sense of okayness in the present moment. A feeling that nothing in particular needs to happen and you're just fine right now, no matter what. It can be a serenity that comes over you when you're doing things you love. Have you ever felt that?

Oneness can be what happens when you are at

the movies and you're so absorbed in the film that you totally lose a sense of your body. You feel like you're totally united with the characters in their plight. Or you can feel oneness when you empathize with someone so much that you shed a tear that rightly belongs to them.

Oneness can also feel deep and spiritual rather than simple, like a wave of warmth and gratitude that sweeps you up as you think about your good luck. Or a sense of quiet happiness when you're praying in church or at a spiritual center of some kind. When you're meditating, you might suddenly feel that your body is warm and alive, as if it's filled with fluffy cotton balls or Squishmallows. And, as odd and uncomfortable as that may sound, it feels incredibly good!

Oneness can come to you like a sense of your boundaries dissolving, as if you don't exist in that moment as *you*, but as a part of the room around you or the location you're dwelling in. You notice, for that moment, that you're united with things around you. And it feels good. It feels carefree. You wouldn't mind if you had a lot more of that sensation in your life. But it will probably happen just for a second, or a few minutes. And then you return to your usual awareness. After all, it's so familiar. You're used to being you.

There's a lot you're here to do as you, and sometimes you lose focus on your oneness. But the more you remain aware of your oneness, that sense of unity with everything comes alive and it feels exactly right.

> "The physical world in many ways is an illusion—especially the illusion of separation."
>
> —DEAN RADIN, PHD

EXPLORATIONS

Feeling Your All-Ness

Sit somewhere where you can see out at least 20 feet in the distance. You could focus on the horizon or simply look up at the sky. Notice how it feels in your body as you take everything in. Do you feel different? More relaxed? Notice the individual objects that you see. You can name them in your mind. Then shift your mindset and think of it all as just one thing. Just one landscape—an entire whole with no division.

Get in touch with that whole, that all-ness. Allow yourself to know that you are also a part of it. As you gaze out into the distance and feel this wholeness, you might notice that the boundaries of your physical body feel less rigid and definite. You may feel more like a part of everything. And your individual worries may feel less prominent.

(Adapted from Rick Hanson's Neurodharma program with permission, RickHanson.com.)

Part Two

Discovering Oneness in Our World

AFFIRMATIONS

I am willing to see the world in a new way.

I know that things are more than they seem and that everything is energy.

In this unified web of life, everything constantly changes and that includes me.

I have unlimited possibilities for becoming new.

> "Black-or-white thinking is a form of cognitive distortion. It is to miss the whole, objective view of something."
>
> —TEAL SWAN

CHAPTER SEVEN

Appreciating the World's Different Perspectives

One of the truly exciting things about growing up is gaining more access to people, cultures, and ideas that are new. Every time your world expands a little, there is a chance to learn and grow. But ask yourself these questions: How open are you to changing your beliefs? Are you willing to see life differently, or are your opinions set in stone?

If you're feeling attached to your current ways of seeing life and yourself, you're in good company. We all sometimes stick to what feels safe and "normal" to us. Yet, as we've been discussing since page one, there are many benefits to seeing things in new ways.

Right now, the people closest to you probably

share many of your basic beliefs about culture, spirituality, and life. As you grow older, though, your world will continue opening up. When this happens, you'll meet more people with different backgrounds and perspectives. You may find some of these people through social media or the internet.

As we've discussed, social media can be a source of negativity and stress, but it also creates amazing opportunities to connect people with differing beliefs and cultures. Technology has helped bring the world closer together, and this is a good thing if we use it right.

As your exposure to different elements in the world grows—for instance, you go to camp, visit your grandparents, hang out more at friends' houses, and eventually attend college—you have a chance to become more interested in the ways of other people. Instead of being afraid of what's different, you can choose to be open-minded and curious about things that don't match your previous ideas.

For instance, maybe your family always cleans the house, but your neighbors hire a house cleaner. That's different! Or maybe your mom cooks elaborate meals, and your friend's mom usually picks something up from a grocery deli or drive-through. Maybe you have a mom and a dad, but your friend has two moms. You can be curious about why people make different choices, with no need to fear or judge what seems different or unusual to you. Maybe, just maybe, there is room for it all to be here and be okay as it is. Nothing has to be wrong or right; it's all just what it is.

How Your Understanding Can Grow

Remember the metaphor of the rock at the lake? If a thousand people stood around the same lake, they would all see something a little different. Everyone's viewpoints would be valid. Still, none of them would be complete. But the more these people talked and shared their views, the greater their collective understanding of the lake would become.

If we embrace the idea of oneness, then we can know that these subtle differences in perceptions and beliefs do not separate us. There is a powerful force that connects us; for this reason, seeing things from new angles does not obstruct our viewpoint but instead widens our perspective.

Instead of perceiving a black-and-white world, with right and wrong (which is really the ego's view), we can expand our minds to include a wider vantage point where more opposing ideas can be respected and valued. To be honest, this even applies to our parents. They are amazing and loving people, but they're not perfect. (Maybe you've noticed?) Neither are your teachers, and that's okay.

As we've been learning, the world is not just one way or another. It's not "my way or the highway," as they say. There is no perfectly right and perfectly wrong way to think, believe, or carry out our lives. Ideally, we can all try to understand each other more and know that there is a place for everything in the spectrum of life. There is a place for all colors, all shapes, all ideas, all beliefs. Life isn't black and white; at the most fundamental level, it is gray.

What is Admirable?

To be sure, our culture often denies this truth, treating certain qualities, traits, and ideas as admirable while devaluing others. For instance, some societies value intelligence (and, alongside it, earning money) as the highest attribute. Other cultures may place way more emphasis on family values and heartfelt connections. In some families and cultures, the only way to appear to be credible may be to believe in a certain religion. For example, a person may need to believe in a certain religion in order to be elected president of a nation.

Different cultures emphasize different things. Something that's considered extremely credible in Western societies, like the United States, is the "scientific paradigm." That term refers to a system for determining reality through scientific methods (like conducting studies, using measurement tools like scales and microscopes, and noticing changes with our eyes). On a societal level, this viewpoint holds more weight than having a creative, mystical, or spiritual viewpoint on life, where the "invisible" or even the "indescribable" is honored.

Most likely, you've noticed that in school, we only learn about the concrete world and what's measurable or provable. We learn that everything is separate and if a well-designed scientific experiment can't verify something, it isn't valid. Ideas that fall outside of this paradigm are deemed fraudulent or iffy at best.

Although this scientific approach, with its reliance on tangible proof, has a lot of value and provides countless benefits, it's only *one method* for determining reality. It's only a tiny part of the human experience—and not even necessarily the most important part. There are many things that are real—love itself being one example—that you can't exactly measure.

And love, you have to admit, is kind of a big deal! Why else would a bazillion songs be written about it?

Examining the Validity of Oneness

Considering the prominence of the scientific view, it is natural to question the validity of oneness as well. I mean, sure, oneness sounds good and everything, like a soft blanket on a winter night, but even so, oneness can seem to be a bit…fluffy. Don't you think?

It wouldn't be too strange if you were asking yourself at this point (or even a few chapters ago) this question: "Is this oneness thing really real? I mean, perhaps it's just a flimsy, idealistic notion embraced by penniless poets and famous hippies (like Rumi and Bob Marley, those guys you were babbling about earlier). Let's get real: Does oneness have any *true* credibility?"

Certainly, it's hard to believe that oneness is fact and not fantasy, because we've never been taught about it. In fact, we've learned the opposite, thanks to the scientific paradigm. We've been taught that everything is separate.

Is there proof of oneness in the greater world? Is oneness really something that is worth believing in? Can this concept stand the test of time? And is there any science to it at all?

To find out, we need to examine oneness from different angles, including what spiritual traditions say about oneness. And even if you don't believe in any form of spirituality right now, which is just fine and perfect as it is, you'll notice that the world has many different traditions that seem to teach similar ideas. You may have to admit that this is intriguing, because they all point to oneness. As you keep your mind open to various points of view, you may discover new and interesting ideas.

> "The problem with black-and-white thinking is that you never get to see the rainbow."
>
> —OMAR SHARIF

EXPLORATIONS

Expanding the Circle of "Us"

Find a comfortable place to sit where you can be relaxed and alert. Gently close your eyes, if you wish. Be aware of your body. Notice how your chest rises and falls with each breath.

Visualize "us." Now bring to mind a group of 2, 3, or 10 people (or more) who really feel like "us" to you: your family, your class, your friend group, your church, etc. Be here with this idea.

Feel that sense of us. What does "us" feel like in your body? Can you get a sense of it? Is it tense, open, closed, warm, cold, fuzzy, sharp, light, heavy?

Begin to open the circle. After you have a sense of what the concept of "us" feels like in your body, try expanding that circle. Begin with who is easy to include in this group of "us." Imagine you're expanding your boundary around "us" to include them. How does that feel in your body? Take a moment to sense that.

Include neutral people. Now, move on to people you don't have strong feelings about. This could include people at your school, or people you haven't thought of as an "us," like neighbors.

Include outsiders. Now, perhaps you can expand your "us" even further, to include people you previously only thought of as a "them"—as being outside of your group. See if you can comfortably do this.

Include everyone. After you've done that, if it feels okay to you, expand your circle to include everyone—omitting no one. Can you find some sense of having common humanity—even with difficult people? For instance: Like me, they want to be liked and loved. Like me, they suffer sometimes. Like me, they want to be happy. Imagine waves of warmth and kindness spreading outward from you to include everyone on Earth, or even beyond. What does this feel like?

(Adapted from "Expanding the Circle of Us" exercise, Neurodharma Program, Rick Hanson, PhD, RickHanson.com)

"There is only one of us.
One consciousness manifesting
into different forms."

—RAM DASS

CHAPTER EIGHT

Spiritual Perspectives on Oneness

THE FIRST PLACE we'll search for proof of oneness is the world's spiritual traditions. Religions have been saying for thousands of years that we are connected with everything, including an all-encompassing spirit or source. And it's not just one religion that's been saying that; it's *all of them*. The world's spiritual traditions all teach very similar concepts—which is a little surprising, because we've been told that spiritual traditions are all so different, to the point where their members even want to fight each other.

But all religions teach love, compassion, and forgiveness—and also our inherent unity as a humanity.

As you'll see in a moment, many of these traditions also describe an underlying oneness that outshines the physical world.

Here are the more prominent religions of the world. The specific stories, details, and star players are different in each religion, but there's a thread running through all of them that connects them to an underlying truth. In his book, *The Essence of the Bhagavad Gita*, Paramahansa Yogananda shares a beautiful analogy to describe this similarity between religions: "Truth is one. People try to slice it like a pie, but even the slices of a pie narrow to a single center."

Buddhism, a spiritual tradition that began in India over 2,500 years ago (and is now popular throughout Asia), teaches that we are interconnected. The Buddha said, "He who experiences the unity of life sees his own self in all beings." Known to have found "enlightenment" through meditation, the Buddha taught that the correct perception of life is that each thing is an intertwined entity, with everything being dependent on everything else for its existence. (This is called "dependent arising.")

The Buddha encouraged the understanding of a "non-self," called anatta. In this way of seeing, we fundamentally do not exist as a separate self, but rather as a collection of experiences. We experience suffering (dukkha) when we cling to those fleeting experiences. Buddhism also casts doubt on the ultimate reality of the physical world, describing a vast "emptiness" that is the deeper reality beneath everything solid we experience with our senses.

Hinduism, a major religion of India, teaches us that the world that we see with our eyes and our five senses is called maya—"illusion"—because it is constantly changing. Therefore, it is not fundamentally real and reliable for providing happiness. A useful analogy is a person who has walked in the desert for a long time sees a mirage in front of them that looks like a pool of water. That person will feel hopeful that it will quench their thirst. However, that mirage can't quench their thirst; similarly, the concrete things of this world can't provide real and lasting happiness. Hinduism also teaches a concept called Brahman, considered to be an overarching God-consciousness. It is sometimes described as "the ultimate reality underlying all phenomena."

Taoism, made popular by the *Tao Te Ching* written in 500 BC, has a main idea called the Tao (pronounced like "the Dow"), which is also sometimes called "the Way." This is an underlying source or energy that forms everything. The goal of Taoism is to act in harmony with this mysterious, all-encompassing source.

Jewish Mysticism, especially the Kabbalist tradition (which began in 12th century Europe), also encourages finding unity with God. God is described as an endless or infinite light, known as Ein Sof. This infinite light manifests in the diverse forms on Earth. This religion also teaches that humans see the world through an illusion of fragmentation, which is referred to as alma de-peruda—translated as "the world of separation."

Sufism, which is an ancient mystical order of Islam, promotes a direct experience and expression of the Divine or God. A concept in Sufism is something called wahdat al-wujūd, or "the Unity of Being," which acknowledges that everything is a unified part of "the one" or God. The poet Rumi, whose poetic wisdom has been widely quoted since he lived 800 years ago, was a Sufi mystic. He expressed a sense of oneness with all of creation in lines such as these: "I am the pang of jealousy, I am the pains of the sick, I am both cloud and rain: I have rained on the meadows."

Christianity refers to the "Trinity," or God manifesting as three things (Father, Son, and Holy

Spirit), and Jesus emphasized treating fellow humans "as yourself." In the Bible, it says, "The Kingdom of Heaven is within you," and some people interpret that to mean that we are one with God and with Heaven. Jesus even said, "I and my father are one," and he affirmed our oneness with him and with God by saying, "Those who believe in me will do the things that I am doing [...] they will do even greater things than these." In **Christian Mysticism,** the ultimate stage to aspire to (through meditation and prayer) is called "unification," which is an experience of uniting with God.

Samadhi is the term used in Buddhism, Hinduism, and Hindu yoga to describe the highest state of awareness a person can attain through meditation or yoga. In this state, the individual's mind merges with Divine consciousness—an experience of unity with all. In Samadhi, "the meditator, the act of meditation, and the object of meditation are finally united."

As you can see, the world's spiritual traditions teach a fundamental unity among all things and with a greater source of life. Regardless of which word they use to refer to that source—whether it's God or Divine or the Tao—they all agree that there is a greater authority beyond the physical world.

"Our perception of what is physical is an illusion. There's nothing physical at all. It's all energy."

—BRUCE H. LIPTON, PHD

EXPLORATIONS

Ball of Light Meditation

An easy way to experience a sense of unity that isn't associated with any certain religion is through the following meditation. When you imagine being surrounded by light, you tap into a deeper truth about life, which is that you are energy and you are part of an interconnected field of energy.

Take a long deep breath, and let it go. As you breathe, try to count to four on each inhale and exhale.

Now try to extend the out-breath for even longer—count to five or six. Notice if you are feeling more relaxed. Let yourself sink into this moment.

On your next out-breath, imagine that your breath flows out and forms a circle of white, radiant, loving light that's enveloping you.

See this beautiful circle of light that you're now surrounded by. What does it look like? It might look like an egg, or the sun, or a huge transparent beach ball, extending many feet outward.

With each out-breath, let your breath flow into this circle of light and fill it up even more. Notice how you feel inside of your body as you sit inside of this light. How far out does it go?

Now imagine that some of your family and friends are there with you, and they also have balls of energy around them. If you have pets or plants you love, see them with balls of energy surrounding them, too.

Now notice that the balls of light extend out from everyone farther and farther. As you all breathe out, the circles of light become bigger and bigger.

Next, imagine that the balls of light extend so far out that they touch each other's borders and blend into each other.

Notice that there are no longer any separate balls of light. They have dissolved and merged into one. Feel that sense of oneness, that merging. How do you feel in your body as you look at this scene?

When you feel complete, you can open your eyes.

"Quantum physics thus reveals a basic oneness of the universe."

—ERWIN SCHRÖDINGER

CHAPTER NINE

Scientific Perspectives on Oneness

WE JUST LOOKED at numerous religions to see how oneness is explained. Still, some people feel that since there is no scientific proof to support these claims, they cannot be accepted as truth. So, let's see what science has to say and how it relates to those ancient beliefs.

The world of science may seem like a strange place to turn to when attempting to verify the truth of our oneness. The fact is, science has been demonstrating for quite a while that we all exist in an interconnected field of energy, and that therefore we affect everything around us in unseen ways.

Physicists who study **quantum physics** focus

on the invisible elements that have an identifiable impact in our world. In the early 1900s, they found that subatomic particles affect each other in strange ways—calling into question our usual way of understanding life and separation.

You see, in classical (or Newtonian) physics, people thought matter was solid and would act in predictable ways when interacting with the laws of nature. But subatomic particles didn't follow those rules.

Quantum Physics Points to Oneness

Picture this. One day, some quantum physicists were conducting an experiment in their lab usual (just doing their uber-exciting scientist thing), and they noticed something strange: After particles interacted with each other and then were separated (similar to what happens in class when students get too chatty), they seemed to *remain* connected somehow. Even when they were separated by a great distance, something odd happened. When one spun in one direction, the other one spun in the other direction, like two sides of a coin. They seemed to still be correlated with each other, as if they were *one unified thing*.

"Why should they still affect each other?" the confused scientists were asking (while also wondering if they'd had enough coffee that morning…or maybe too much?). It defied the known laws of physics at the time.

Since then, this weirdness has been verified countless times, and it's now an undisputed phenomenon called "nonlocality" or "quantum entanglement." (PS: The implications of this discovery are still being unraveled.)

At first, quantum entanglement seemed to be an unexplainable oddity. In fact, Albert Einstein was confused by it, calling it a "spooky action at a distance." Now, however, it makes a little more sense. This is because scientists have now discovered that particles are part of a vast underlying sea of energy called a field, and everything is encompassed by this larger energetic ocean. It's almost as if subatomic particles are miniscule cell phones connected by a huge cellular network. Particles don't exist alone like hermits; they're automatically engaged with others in a lively dialogue, because they're embedded in a constantly vibrating, communicating web.

Inside of this web, it turns out that things aren't totally solid. Everything keeps changing. Scientists now know that, in certain circumstances, *all particles* (those little dots) *are also waves* (like spread-out packets of energy).

Initially, this discovery was a bit shocking, because scientists thought energy (waves) and things (particles) were very different, but it turns out that everything is actually *both*! This is "wave-particle duality."

In fact, get this: It's possible that we actually *create reality* as we—our minds—interact with this underlying field of energy, particles, and waves. This is called "the observer effect," which scientists discovered because they realized that particles didn't decide to be particles until they were viewed by someone. Or, at least it sure seemed that way.

You see, scientists started to notice that a particle only became solid and measurable at the exact instant they observed it. Prior to this, it was a fuzzy little wave of energy called a wave packet. But at the very millisecond they zeroed in on it with their fancy equipment, the spread-out wave packet seemed to magically transform itself into a solid particle. And it kept happening this way. This rocked their worlds! This phenomenon is now called "collapse of the wave packet."

It became clear that we are *not* innocent bystanders, watching life unfold. Instead, we help create reality by interacting with the world. Some might even say that our perceptions, or our minds—or what some people call our *consciousness*—literally shape the world that we see and experience.

Phew! Obviously, all the details on this can fill a whole shelf of textbooks (and if you're curious, you can go to your local bookstore or see the recommended reading list at the end of this book for more great sources). But here's the basic gist of what science shows us about oneness (and if the previous bullet points turned your mind into a ball of putty, just note these takeaways):

It turns out that everything is interconnected by a huge web (through an underlying field that has uncanny similarities to the "God" or all-encompassing Source, Light, Flow, or Energy described by spiritual traditions). And that even solid things that we see in front of us are also "energy."

Nothing is fixed in a certain state; it's all in flux. And we can affect or create reality with our minds.

You can see why one Nobel Prize-winning physicist, Werner Heisenberg, concluded that rather than anything being "real," it's all just potential. He said, "The atoms or elementary particles themselves are not real; they form a world of potentialities or possibilities." Elementary particles are like that, we are like that, and our lives are like that.

Could it be true?

Discoveries like those I just mentioned have made it increasingly clear that we are all intertwined, we all affect each other, and we can change our reality by how we view it. We are in a state, in the words of the Buddha, of "inter-being" with everything.

Other Proof of Oneness

Many areas of science have revealed that we do create our reality and have a connection to everything. Because of this, we can produce a change in our world instantaneously and often unknowingly. The fact that the aforementioned observer effect, nonlocality, quantum entanglement, and this web of oneness is really *real* is the reason why the following things have been shown to be true:

It's the reason we think of someone we haven't talked to for a while *right before* they text us.

It's the reason for "the placebo effect," which is when people heal from a condition simply because they believe they are receiving healing when, in reality, they are being given sugar pills or "sham"— aka fake—surgery.

It's why people can know that they are being stared at, even from behind. (Have you noticed this?)

It's the reason people have cured themselves of health conditions—even "incurable" cancer—by repeatedly imagining that they are healing using specific techniques.

It's why praying for sick people has been shown to work (especially if a group prays).

It's behind the discovery of mirror neurons, which are cells in the brain that react *exactly* the same way when *we* take a certain action (like pick up a cup) as they do when witnessing *another* person take that same action.

It's the reason that pregnant women's partners often feel many of the same symptoms they are feeling—even having nausea, weight gain, and belly cramps! This strange occurrence even has a medical name: Couvade syndrome.

It's why a recent study showed that people who ghost others via text or social media tend to feel worse in the subsequent time period, often feeling depressed.

Astronomy, Astrophysics, and Oneness

Other branches of science that highlight our interconnectedness include astrophysics and astronomy. Astrophysicists have discovered that we are made out of the dust from dying stars. "We are literally made out of star stuff," explains astrophysicist Suzanna Randall. And astronomers in New Mexico surveyed the stars in 2017, confirming that, in fact, we share 97% of the same atoms (smaller-than-microscopic particles) with stars.

If you think about it, this shouldn't be that surprising. Everything is made of the same basic building blocks because we are created by and connected to each and every thing by that unifying "web." Famous astrophysicist Neil deGrasse Tyson explains how this connection can feel empowering: "I look up at the night sky and I know that, yes, we are part of this Universe, we are in this Universe, but perhaps more important than both of those facts is that the Universe is in us. When I reflect on that fact, I look up—many people feel small, because they're small and the Universe is big, but I feel big, because my atoms came from those stars."

Perhaps even more interestingly, there are some who believe we are *re-formed* with *new* stardust every few years. Astrophysicist Karel Schrijver and his wife Iris wrote in their book *Living with the Stars*, "Thus, we are not merely connected to the universe in some distant sense: stardust from the universe is actually flowing through us on a daily basis, and it rebuilds the stars and planets throughout the universe as much as it does our bodies, over and over again." So, we never have to be stuck, or fixed, in our realities. Everything is changing, including our entire selves!

What's the takeaway? When we talk about oneness, you can know it's not just an imaginary idea that sounds cool (or just plain weird). It's proven, and it's real. And more evidence is accumulating all the time.

The potential for this is significant as you learn how to use this new mindset to transform your world. Step by step, you will discover how to create a newly harmonious, unconditionally happy life that is aligned with the true workings of the Universe. You're here for a reason, and you deserve to have so many beautiful opportunities to make your life a sweet dream come true.

"Quantum physicists have found that there is one consciousness with which we can all connect, of which we all are a part. You can call it the Holy Spirit, you can call it the Tao, or The Way."

—FREDERICK CHAVALIT TSAO

EXPLORATIONS

Reflection

Does oneness seem more credible to you now? Is there something in particular about this chapter that convinced you there might really be something to it?

Consider what it would mean to you if you were able to "let go" and "grow into" a new way of seeing yourself and the situation.

For example, "I can let go of the physical problems that have been bothering me and grow into a healthy, radiant person who confidently steps forward into the world."

"It is a scientific fact that what is good for you is good for me."

—DR. DAVID HAWKINS

CHAPTER TEN

Oneness Helps Create a More Harmonious World

ADOPTING AND LIVING a life based on a oneness perspective doesn't only benefit ourselves; it also benefits the greater world. When we feel more positive and complete within ourselves, that radiates out to others far and wide. Our feeling states broadcast to others because we exist in a unified web of life that can be described as a gigantic "psychic internet," a term coined by science writer Lynne McTaggart.

It's like we're all constantly connected to an underlying network. Because we belong to a web of life, our thoughts and emotions influence the greater world. When we feel a sense of unity, compassion, empathy, and well-being, we positively influence others in that moment, even if we don't realize it.

Also, when we truly feel unified, we act in new ways that benefit the greater whole. We do things differently. We are more aware of others. We're willing to lend a hand and offer a smile. As our inner world becomes harmonious, we start to make the world better.

Nobel-prize-winning physicist David Bohm, author of *Wholeness and the Implicate Order*, said that believing we are separate creates every single problem in society. This illusion, he said, "cannot do other than lead to endless conflict and confusion." He said that this idea "has led to the growing series of extremely urgent crises that is confronting us today." (I'm sure you can think of a few of those!)

The alternative viewpoint Bohm offered was that, "Ultimately, the entire universe [...] has to be understood as a single undivided whole." As everyone learns more about our inherent oneness and acts in alignment with that knowledge, we will find our world transforming into a much better place. The problems that people's past ego-dominated actions caused (such as wars, discrimination, pollution, and global warming) will disappear.

A mindset that emphasizes separation, after all, is a dangerous one. Rick Hanson, the psychologist I mentioned before, explains that the minute we separate things into "us" and "them," we are stoking a fire that often ends in discrimination and wars.

When we believe we are separate, we get stressed out, and our minds can go off the rails. We get funny ideas, like that we should start wars with people who look and think differently than us or have different priorities than us. We dislike people who have what we wish we had. We divide others into good and bad, and even divide ourselves into good and bad parts.

You can see evidence of this on social media and other online comment threads. In those forums, people are determined to view the world in a separatist way, distinguishing bad from good. What does that result in? It results in people attacking each other, saying how "wrong," "stupid," "ugly," "ignorant," and "rude" other people are.

People even dislike others who are on different sports teams, simply because they are on the opposing team through no real fault of their own. People often forget that the other team has all the same hopes, dreams, and feelings that our team does. Why is one group more important to us than the other?

As soon as we divide people into "us and them" we already have allowed a false sense of separation to begin breeding suspicion, aloofness, mistrust, and even—eventually—hatred.

It doesn't have to be this way. We can be part of a worldwide awakening. We can be the ones to change our minds about life and see things differently, shine our positive lights on the world, and infuse it with the perspective that heals: We are all one.

> "At the deepest sub-nuclear level, you and I are literally ONE."
>
> —JOHN HAGELIN

EXPLORATIONS

Reflection

Do the people around you have a oneness mindset or not? In what ways do you see people exhibiting oneness or the opposite?

What is one way you could help bring more of a oneness mindset to these situations in your life?

Part Three

Putting Your Oneness Into Practice

AFFIRMATIONS

I easily find the path that's right for me,
I trust in the Universe's plan,
I surrender to my highest good,
I forgive myself and others,
and I know that life will provide me with
new and wonderful experiences!

> "Don't you know yet?
> It's your light that lights the world."
>
> —RUMI

CHAPTER ELEVEN

Utilizing Oneness to Find Your Purpose

MOST RELIGIOUS OR SPIRITUAL TRADITIONS, if they have anything to say about why we are here, proclaim that we are here to love. To love others and to receive love from others. Explains Sue Morter, author of *The Energy Codes*, "Our life experience is about discovering love and infusing it into all we do."

Love?!? Too simple, right? What about grades, careers, chores, social media likes, pleasing people, gaining an education, or developing important skills? At least *some* of those things matter, don't they? Sure, they matter to some extent, but underneath it all, when all's said and done, what matters most in our lives is the love we give and receive.

Even if love truly is the only thing we are *really* here for, why *you*, specifically? Anyone can love, right? Why are *you* here with all your uniqueness?

Some say that there is a creator of everything—whether you call that God, Spirit, Life, Light, or the Universe (in this book, we're just calling it Universe). This original source delivered each of us to this Earth for a *reason*. From this perspective, *your* life is as important as every other life on Earth. Even people who are famous or do amazing things are not any more important than you. And by the way, being famous doesn't make you happy. It just makes you famous. Being famous can be good or it can be bad. Everything is in your state of mind.

On the other side of the spectrum, people who've done terrible things aren't any worse than you. They just had different influences and made certain choices. From this viewpoint, you've been purposely created as a unique element of life. Your life has an important purpose, mission, or reason for being (raison d'être, in French). You fulfill it just by being here and being you. *Zen Teen* author and angel expert Tanya Carroll Richardson describes one way to think about it: "The angels tell me we are all loved and 'treasured' equally. And we are all important—'vital'—without exception. Otherwise, you would not exist at all."

For more proof of your importance, consider the words of the late Wayne W. Dyer, bestselling author of so many enlightening books: "It's impossible for you not to belong, because your presence here is evidence that a divine universal Source intended you here."

In case that wasn't enough to convince you, here's what Matt Kahn, spiritual teacher and author of *Whatever Arises, Love That,* says: "Every heart is the missing piece that completes the puzzle of the Universe."

We're not here by accident or by chance. We're meant to be here. We may not understand all the reasons why, but our existence matters.

Finding Purpose and Flow

How do we find those reasons why we're here, though? How do we discover our own purpose? You fulfill your purpose just by being the person you are. You also fulfill it when you are doing those things only you can do in your unique way. When you do the things that you find so absorbing and satisfying that you can't stop (or wouldn't want to stop) doing them, you're fulfilling your purpose (as long as they're wholesome, not destructive, things!).

Another way to think of it is that you're fulfilling your purpose when you do the activities that feel *so* natural to you, it feels like breathing. When you do them, you feel "in the flow" of life. Everything feels exactly right at that very moment.

An entire book was written about this phenomenon called "flow" (which, fittingly, is that book's title). It's when you are so engaged in something that your focus is completely absorbed—to the point where you lose a sense of time and space.

This differs from losing track of time by escaping into addictive time-sucking activities like scrolling social media threads, which don't always feel truly uplifting or nourishing. You can tell by how you feel afterward. Do you feel better or worse than you did before? Do you feel more complete and whole, or less so?

When you do things that promote this positive sense of flow, they should feel very "full" and engaging in a way that makes you feel the most "you" that you can ever feel. You feel lost in the moment, yet in touch with the core of yourself.

Do you know what those things are for you? What are you compelled to do?

What makes you feel totally "right," totally at home in the world?

Which (positive and healthy) activities help you feel better?

What puts you in touch with your true self, or at least what feels like it *might* be your true self?

What things do you do that make you feel you are "in the flow," so much that you lose a sense of time, or even a sense of your physical boundaries?

You are supposed to be doing those things, being those things, and just expressing *you*.

We Have a Destiny

Beyond that, some even say we have a *destiny* in our lives, something we are purposely here for. Some believe there is a predestined plan that's in place when we are born. That's kind of a cool idea, isn't it? If so, then things aren't random and meaningless. There's a purpose and a plan.

Maybe we are destined to work in a certain profession or marry a certain person. Maybe *we* are the ones to solve certain problems around us, or to be the voice of reason. Perhaps we are here to be the eyes, ears, or voice of compassion that the world is calling for.

Destiny isn't something people commonly talk about in Western culture. The truth is, everywhere you turn, people have differing opinions on whether our lives are destined to be a certain way or are solely ours to shape (or a little of both). What is the truth?

Perhaps greater sources of wisdom, like esteemed writers and published spiritual texts, can shed some light on this issue. Since spiritual traditions helped us discover some truths about oneness, let's see if they can enlighten us about destiny as well.

Eastern Religion and Destiny

Eastern religions, such as Buddhism and Hinduism, share the belief that we have a destiny of some sort. Our destinies, in these traditions, are influenced by what is called "karma." Karma is like a universal accounting system that tallies up the pluses and minuses of all our past actions. This tally is then used to determine our life circumstances in the future. Karma ensures that "what comes around, goes around" or "we reap what we sow," because our actions and intentions have a ripple effect in the universe for quite a while (some say forever).

As author and psychologist Rick Hanson comically explains, "Karma is like hitting a golf ball in the shower." This rather ill-advised and painful-sounding metaphor suggests something important: You might think you're sending your actions and words out to other people, but they bounce back and impact you.

In the belief of Eastern religions, this tally also carries into our next lives when we're reincarnated in a new body. The topic of whether we're reincarnated is too much to ponder in this little book, so I'll leave that exploration up to you.

The karma theory suggests that we are born with certain conditions that result from past karma. This includes being born into a certain geographical area with a certain family and circumstances, as well as specific personal attributes. Part of our destiny entails resolving this past karma, as well as creating new positive karma that ensures positive future conditions for us.

How do we resolve any bad karma? We reverse it through benevolent intentions and actions. As we act with kindness, nobility, and equality, we start to dissolve the bad karma. We also develop spiritually, reaching higher levels of awareness and compassion for all beings, which in Eastern traditions is the whole point of life.

Admittedly, karma can be a haunting concept, especially when we recall the times when we tortured a sibling, gossiped about friends, or excluded an innocent person. But don't worry; the situation isn't as grim as it sounds. Our karma is never set in stone. We can influence it and regain control of our destiny by co-creating with new intentions, thoughts, and actions. Sadhguru, a popular yoga teacher and author from India who wrote *Karma: A Yogi's Guide to Crafting Your Destiny*, explains, "The spiritual practice is, by definition, always about taking your destiny in your own hands."

Jay Shetty, author of *Think Like a Monk*, explains that in Buddhist philosophy we all have a dharma, which is our purpose in life. "Your dharma is already within you. It's always been with you. It's woven into your being," he explains. Perhaps part of our karma is our dharma, and we will eventually discover what that is.

Christianity and Destiny

Just as Eastern religions seem to point toward the existence of destiny, the Bible is filled with instances of people being selected for certain destinies and receiving instructions about their fates. According to the stories, this is usually communicated in visions or dreams. The Bible also provides instructions on how to discover our destinies: by dwelling in a space of quiet and solitude in order to hear this ever-present guidance.

Does This Apply to Me?

If religious traditions provide any indication, some people seem to have destinies. However, it can be difficult to know if this applies to the rest of us. Maybe destinies are just for the special "chosen" ones?

Many esteemed teachers have claimed that destiny is not just for a few of us; that, in fact, we all have destinies. Florence Scovel Shinn, a popular metaphysical author and teacher in the early 1900s, wrote that she believed we all have destinies and that we contain information about our destinies inside of us.

In her book, *Your Word is Your Wand*, Shinn reassures us that "Just as the perfect picture of the oak is in the acorn, the divine pattern of his [or her] life is in the superconscious [or Divine] mind of [wo]man."

From this viewpoint, our job is less to *discover* our purpose as it is to remove the blocks to what we *already know* beneath our usual awareness. We're drawn to certain things for a reason, almost as if our interests were planted there from the beginning, like a smart little acorn that knows the way the tree is supposed to grow.

The Artist's Way author Julia Cameron says that what you loved to do when you were 10 years old or younger can be a clue to an important life passion. When you were younger, you just did certain enjoyable activities without thinking, simply because you felt like it and because those activities felt right inside of you. And there can be many things like that; not just one.

This was before you started conforming to the world, feeling you had to "get serious" and do what everyone else was doing. Maybe you scoped out the competition and gave up. Perhaps someone didn't respond positively, and you started doubting yourself. Still, you shouldn't forget what you knew about yourself from the very beginning.

Often, how we chose to play when we were young can reveal our innate values, tendencies, and interests. If you don't remember how you spent your time as a child, ask your parents or caregivers. This doesn't have to just point to a career; your early activities can also point to fulfilling hobbies that will always bring joy to your life.

Anita Moorjani, author of *Dying to Be Me* and *Sensitive is the New Strong*, agrees that we all have a destiny. She learned from her near-death experience (in which she technically died and then came back to life with fully regenerated health) that our destined path represents the greatest possible outcome of our lives. "The difference between our destiny and our free will," she explains, "is that our destiny is our highest potential, but we have the free will as to whether we want to attain it or not."

To discover our destiny, we must tune in to our inner life, says Moorjani. "Dreams and wishes and imagination are your connection to your truth," she notes. "They are the insights about who you desired to come here to be."

She counsels that, "We have to listen to our inner voice. We've made the voice of the world stronger than our inner voice. We have to change that."

Shinn offers this great affirmation to help you discover your destined path: "The Divine Design of my life now comes to pass. I now fill the place that I can fill and no one else can fill. I now do the things which I can do and no one else can do."

Your destiny path can feel like a puzzle you'll never be able to solve, but Jay Shetty consoles us by saying that "Our dharmas [or destinies] don't hide, but sometimes we need to work patiently to recognize them." It can simply take a little time and persistence. They tend to reveal themselves to us along the way. All we need to do is notice.

Finding Purpose by Overcoming Difficulties

Sometimes you'll figure out what you're meant to do simply by being in the process of overcoming difficulties, such as having inspiration while sorting through some painful feelings. After you surmount a challenge, you might think, *I made it through this. Now I want to help others get through this type of thing, too.*

Everyone has difficulties in life, but the question is: What will you do with them?

Some people turn their difficulties into music; others turn them into another type of creative art. Some turn them into helping others in their professional life as doctors, counselors, researchers, nutritionists, ministers, or other types of healers. Becoming a parent is also something that can be transformative and healing.

Sometimes you can't find your truest calling until you go through something that throws your whole world off-kilter. In the midst of it, you just suddenly *know* your passion and path. It could seem like a big realization or a small one, and it could happen at any age—at 10, 18, or 45. (You might even go through several of them.)

There's no timeline you need to meet. In college, you have to choose your area of focus (your major), but you may not know what you *really* want to do until later. It might have zero to do with your major! One study found that only 27 percent of people have jobs related to their majors.

You've probably heard that J. K. Rowling, author of the Harry Potter series, didn't publish her first book until she was 32 after receiving 12 rejections from publishers. Famous chef Julia Child didn't start cooking until she was 32 and published her first cookbook at age 49. So just know that you've got *lots* of time to figure all this out!

Being in Harmony

When we talk about finding our destinies and creating our lives, it's good to remember that we need to do it in a way that feels natural, not overly forced. When you make a move (whether it's a class to take or a friend to make), make a move that feels like it is in harmony with the whole universe. That may sound like a tall order, but it's basically the move that feels best. You might be the only one who thinks it's a good move. Deep inside, though, it feels right to you and it feels like it is "in sync" with the moon and stars.

The more you do what is natural, not forced—the more you do what feels almost like you didn't even *try* to do it, it was like breathing to do that thing—the more you are on the right track.

Earlier, I mentioned the experience of flow. Others might call it being "in the zone." In the 2020 Pixar movie *Soul*, the main character Joe, who is middle-aged, goes to the afterlife and learns that humans need to find their "spark," which is "that thing you're born to do." Then he is brought to The Zone, described as "the space between the spiritual and physical." This Zone is the place humans go to when they are enjoying what they are doing so much that they are transported to "another place."

When Joe plays piano, he is shown entering that Zone, which is as if he is suspended somewhere between the physical (Earth realm) and spiritual (Heaven, or Universe, or, as this movie refers to it, "The Great Beyond"). This is an experience we want to be on the lookout for.

An important lesson Joe learns in the movie, though, is that he shouldn't *only* focus on pursuing his passion and purpose; he should also notice the miracle of every moment—even the wonder of a tiny helicopter seed falling from the sky into his palm.

Following the Tao

This state of wonder and alignment with the Universe is explained in certain religions such as Taoism. In Taoism, the goal of life is to act in harmony with an all-encompassing force called the Tao, which is an energy that is the source and substance of everything (similar to "the field" discovered by quantum physics or what we're calling Universe).

Taoism and books such as the ancient Taoist text the *Tao Te Ching* state that the wise person acts with naturalness and spontaneity and achieves "perfection" by becoming one with the unplanned rhythms of the Universe. Lao Tzu states, "At the center of your being you have the answer; you know who you are, and you know what you want."

In this state, you're not so much forcing or resisting things, which most of us are inclined to do as we attempt to control our environment. Instead, you're moving serenely, in sync with the natural flow of life, knowing just how to stay in harmony with the whole. You let go of resistance, and you become open to the wonder of the moment. You don't take action until you feel called to do so.

To act from a still, quiet, and calm place inside may come from recognizing that you are a part of everything, and that the trees, the rocks, the dirt, and the streams are all really connected to you. This wisdom might even just hit you when you are in nature and really feeling good. It almost feels like you *are* the fresh air, you *are* the sunshine, you *are* the deer in the field, you *are* the ocean. You can feel this oneness and merging with nature anytime you are spending time outdoors. You've probably felt that way at least once, if not many times.

There's a reason for this. In the words of spiritual teacher and author Eckhart Tolle: "We are not separate from nature. We are all part of the *one* life that manifests itself in countless forms throughout the universe, forms that are all completely interconnected."

Being One with the Whole

Keeping this in mind, always make sure that whatever you pursue in life helps contribute to the happiness of everything on earth. "Progress" of any kind that destroys the health of anything else on Earth is *not* really progress at all!

It seems self-evident, doesn't it? But in the quest for popularity, fame, money, and power, people forget this!

It's good to remember that everything on Earth has dependent relationships with everything else. We need healthy soil for growing food, the fish need clean water as their habitat, the animals need trees for shade and shelter, and we all need clean air. Also, we need all the other people on Earth to help us get what we need in our daily lives.

The more we are all feeling in harmony with the Tao, the more we are all helping each other live in a peaceful, prosperous world. When you are in this state of mind, amazing things can happen. You start to feel like you "just know" what is about to happen (like who is going to contact you), and you may feel like eerie coincidences keep happening. That thing you wanted may just suddenly show up on your doorstep or, out of the blue, someone will tell you something that solves your problem. You are in harmony with everything, and it feels like things are working out amazingly!

"Infinite Spirit, open the way for the Divine Design of my life to manifest; let the genius within me now be released; let me see clearly the perfect plan."

—FLORENCE SCOVEL SHINN

EXPLORATIONS

Breath-Counting Meditation

They say that the wisdom, flow, and Tao of the Universe can be found in stillness. You can contact this stillness through breath-counting meditation.

Find a comfortable, quiet spot and make an intention to focus on your breath and let your thoughts, plans, ideas, and your to-do list fall away.

1. Breathe in and out. Inhale through your nose and then exhale out through your mouth to the count of 1. Inhale again, then out to the count of 2, and try to get to 10 before you find yourself wandering.

2. Stay focused. When you notice that you just started thinking about something else and have lost focus on your counting, start back at 1 again.

3. Keep counting as you breathe and try to stay in that still, beautiful, clear-minded, peaceful state. Do your best for 5 or 10 minutes and try to see if you can count higher next time.

"Soul is spirit. In quantum science, soul is information. Soul, spirit, and information are the same."

—ZHI GANG SHA, MD

CHAPTER TWELVE

Tuning In to Your Inner Compass

Each day you wake up and are confronted by many choices: Whether to obey your alarm and get out of bed, or to keep hitting snooze. You decide what to eat for breakfast, what to wear, and what to bring with you when you leave the house. Mentally, you are already preparing for the situations you'll be facing, and you are making decisions about how you'll probably handle them.

After school or work, you face more choices: How long to spend on screens, whom to message, what type of snack to have *(Four bowls of cereal again? Heck yes!)*, and what to do with your time. Sometimes it's hard to know if you are making the right choices.

What standards should guide your choices? Is it just "what feels easiest"—like maybe the no-homework thing—or "what Grandma would approve of," which might be actually *doing* the homework?

Even on social media, you can feel unsure:

Should I do a post about my new pet goldfish? I mean, he's pretty cute!

But I wonder if I am posting too much lately.

Should I stop posting my super-moody poetry—which is kind of brilliant, if you ask me? Does anyone care?

Should I have replied to Amanda's post, or is a "like" enough to keep her happy?

Honestly, you can make yourself a little crazy. And, sure, if you're 18 or younger, your parents probably make a lot of your choices. If you're in school, your teachers and school make a lot of choices for you too. But there are always small choices to make, and, as you get older, every year you'll have *more* choices and bigger decisions to make. Before you know it, you'll be the number-one person steering the ship of your life. *Where* will you steer it? Toward beautiful destinations, or through several stormy seas?

Even more importantly, *how* will you steer it? What kind of GPS will you be using?

The "Doing what your family always did" GPS?

The "Doing what friends think you should do" GPS?

The "Rebellion" GPS, which chooses the opposite path of what you're "supposed to" choose?

Or the "Inner Truth Compass" GPS, which leads to the things that are exactly right for you?

The Inner Truth Compass

It's easy sometimes to just "let life happen," to act without thinking, to go along with the crowd. If your friends do certain things, you do them too to fit in. We all want to be accepted and to feel like we are a part of something. But when we make decisions with that type of guidance system (which is basically autopilot mode), the things we do don't always *feel* like they're really right for us…not deep down inside, anyway. They might even end up feeling downright wrong and they could bring some unwanted consequences, too.

Did you know that there's a part of yourself that is always in touch with the *right* thing to do?

It's your *intuition*!

Sometimes people call it your "inner voice."

It's that thing where you have a "hunch" about

something—you just *know* something, but you don't know *how* you know it! Some call it a "gut feeling." Something doesn't feel quite right in the pit of your stomach.

Or maybe something just feels right and you notice a light, airy feeling inside and warmth all over. It's like, *Yeah, I just know this is it!*

But where does that "voice" or sense come from?

Some say it's the wise part of yourself—your inner guidance, your "higher self," or God or Spirit within you or speaking to you from outside of you. You may even just say it's the "greater knowing" that is part of a collective field of wisdom (aka Universe). But does anyone know what intuition *really* is?

What is Intuition?

The dictionary defines intuition as "the ability to understand something immediately, without the need for conscious reasoning." Bill Bennett, author of *PGS: Intuition is Your Personal Guidance System*, offers a similar definition: "Intuition is the sudden, unexplained insight that comes unaided by logic, intellect, or expertise."

You may wonder, though: What gives us the ability to have those kinds of "unexplained insights"? The answer is that we have that ability because we are connected to a greater oneness—an all-encompassing source. We are interconnected with others, and we are also connected with an infinite source of wisdom.

As we talked about in Part 2, scientists have discovered an underlying field of energy that connects everything in the Universe. Since everything merges with this field, the field contains all the wisdom and information about anything you could want to know. David Bohm, the brilliant and forward-thinking quantum physicist we discussed earlier, developed a theory that explained how this works.

He divided our reality into two parts, the one we can see, smell, and touch and another that is a higher, more "energetic" dimension. This higher dimension, he proposed, holds all the information and intelligence of our world within it.

In some ways, this higher dimension is the truer reality, Bohm explained. He described how this dimension worked: It pulses information down into our concrete, three-dimensional physical world. Then these pulsating events are perceived by us innocent bystanders as the solid world around us. These pulses happen so quickly that we see things as concrete and real, but it's all energy.

He also said the world was a holograph—a three-dimensional picture (similar to a laser holographic image) in which each part contains the whole. The higher dimension can pulsate everywhere at once, causing everything to be fused and related to each other. Basically, in Bohm's words, you're a holograph, containing the whole.

Hundreds of years ago, the poet Rumi knew the interconnectedness that scientists have described. He expressed it in this way: "You are not a drop in the ocean. You are the entire ocean in a drop."

The Information That Surrounds Us

Many authors have explained this interconnectedness and resulting automatic exchange of energy. In her fascinating book, *The Field: The Quest for the Secret Force of the Universe*, science writer Lynne McTaggart explains the quantum physics of intuition this way: "On our most fundamental level, living beings, including human beings, were [being proven to be] packets of quantum energy constantly exchanging information with this inexhaustible energy sea."

Guided imagery expert Belleruth Naparstek describes it similarly in her book, *Your Sixth Sense*, in which she summarizes Bohm's findings: "The world appears solid and three-dimensional, but [...] it really pulsates with intelligence that is nonlocal—everywhere at once—and that holds all of time in a co-present fashion [...] Again, because everything is enfolded within everything else, this vast information field is everywhere, inside of us and outside of us."

Mind-blowing, right?

This theory from Bohm helps us understand intuition in a more scientific way. Intuition exists because we are all interconnected with each other and with a greater source of information and intelligence. Is this making sense yet?

Famous psychologist Carl Jung called this vast storehouse of information the "collective unconscious," which is like all our minds joined together and combined with the "cosmic mind." He explained that in addition to the thoughts and ideas in our own personal consciousness, "there exists a second psychic system of a collective, universal, and impersonal nature which is identical in all individuals. When we have ideas, motivations, and inspirations, we are not the only one responsible; we are also under the influence of a unified consciousness that is greater than ourselves."

Enlisting Your Ally

To be sure, this science can be a bit mind-boggling. The point is, there is a place within all of us that is in touch with an abundance of information and intelligence. This is our intuition. It may help to think of your intuition as a tiny person who lives within you and is always connected to that huge information field. You can think of this person as your inner ally, your personal assistant, or your BFF.

And this BFF is a good one indeed. They have nothing else to do and no one else they want to hang out with. They are devoted to your well-being—and yours alone. They know you better than anyone, and they can be *really* honest.

They are also protective. And they will yell loudly to get your attention and keep you away from danger. They are totally different from your ego.

They might say things like:

Go to that party. It will be good for you!

Join that club. You'll love it!

Don't go along with what those girls are doing—their ideas aren't right for you.

Make friends with Sarah! She's the true, loyal friend you deserve.

Don't eat those cheese fries—your stomach will regret it!

They may not literally say those things in words, but you'll get the message coming from inside of you somewhere. You'll feel it, or you may have a sense of "No" or "Don't you do *that*, girl!" You may even have a dream that feels like it contains a warning message, and that's your intuition speaking too.

It's hard to acknowledge and heed these subtle messages that come to us, because we aren't encouraged to pay attention to them. Western society values a logical, rational, thought-out approach most. But relying on your brain as your only guide can be limiting. Your brain may be your best ally in certain situations, like figuring out math problems, remembering poems, and recalling the right notes to play on the piano. Having good manners and saying the right thing can also come from a sense of right and wrong, which you've learned over time.

Yet, if you want to know the *best* thing to do when you're faced with a decision that you can freely make, your BFF Intuition's got your back! The answer may not "make sense," but it may lead you to exactly where you're meant to be.

On the other hand, it may make perfect sense. Your brain and your intuition don't have to be in disagreement. If you use them as a team, you'll find your life working out quite well! Often it's good to do some research and confirm your intuitions with some real-world data and input.

Of course, sometimes "life happens," and things aren't working out well…but that is an opportunity to find the intuitive way forward toward a better day.

Why We Need Intuition

People often think of those people who are living super-intuitive lives as being a little bit magical. We often have an image of wise old sages wielding witchcraft, like the Sanderson sisters in *Hocus Pocus*.

Relegating intuition to strange old ladies might work in the movies, but intuition is here for all of us to use—even when we're young. In fact, during the teen and young adult years, there are many reasons why it's particularly important to use this guidance.

A pioneer in the field of psychology, Erik Erikson, named this stage during the preteen and teen years "Identity vs. Role Confusion." During this stage, it's time to establish an identity as a separate individual. If you are on autopilot or just do what others say, you won't have a chance to develop your identity and may remain stuck in "role confusion," not knowing exactly who you are.

On the other hand, your brain at this stage has a tendency to get overwhelmed by your emotions, which overshadow the prefrontal cortex or "good decision-making" part of your brain. If you just do whatever compels you, without caring about the consequences, you can end up with something more than an identity—you can get yourself into a load of trouble!

So, calming yourself and finding a way to use your intuition—which comes from a place that is outside of the brain and emotions—can be a great way to make decisions right now.

It's also a great way to find your own unique place in the world. You can't necessarily expect to know exactly what you want to do career-wise yet, but you can follow the clues to realize who you really are, what matters to you, and the things in this world that fit you best.

Many successful people swear by intuition as the best road map in life. In the words of Madeleine L'Engle, author of the incredible book *A Wrinkle in Time*: "Don't try to comprehend with your mind. Your minds are very limited. Use your intuition."

Bestselling author Deepak Chopra shares this axiom: "To know without thinking is the highest intelligence."

And, in case that isn't enough to convince you, one of the greatest thinkers who ever lived, Albert Einstein—who obviously used the ol' cranium for *a lot* of productive work—had this to say: "The only real valuable thing is intuition."

You can't really argue with Albert Einstein, can you? He's got some clout!

By now, hopefully you're convinced that intuition can be a helpful force in your life. In the next chapter, you'll learn more about exactly how to use this guidance.

> "Intuition comes out of being present."
>
> —ECKHART TOLLE

EXPLORATIONS

Quick Coherence® Technique

The HeartMath® Institute offers this quick exercise that can bring you instantly into a state of better alignment with your inner guidance, putting you into a confident, calm, good-feeling state. And it only takes a minute to do!

1. Focus your attention on the area of the heart. Imagine your breath is flowing in and out of your heart or chest area, breathing a little slower and deeper than usual. Find an easy rhythm that's comfortable.
2. As you continue heart-focused breathing, make a sincere attempt to experience a regenerative feeling, such as appreciation or care for someone or something in your life.

QUICK STEPS

1. Heart-focused breathing
2. Activate a positive or renewing feeling.

(Used by permission of HeartMath® Institute.)

"Intuition is the whisper of the soul."

—J. KRISHNAMURTI

CHAPTER THIRTEEN

Following Your Intuition

YOU MAY BE THINKING, *"Sure, sounds cool, but…um …excuse me, how exactly do I follow my intuition?"* The first step in following your intuition is to listen more closely to *you*, which involves spending more time giving yourself silent, focused attention.

"Being silent? And focusing on myself? No thanks!" you may be (understandably) thinking.

If you're not used to sitting quietly for periods of time, it can seem kind of weird or scary.

The truth is, it can be relaxing and satisfying. You don't have to sit there straight as a rod chanting "Ohhhmmm," while probing your mind for deep, dark secrets. It can be easy and pleasant. You don't even have to sit up; you can lie down and get comfortable. You can also, of course, download a meditation playlist or use a meditation app.

If you're thinking that being quiet and still isn't productive, think about Einstein. He was always sitting around in a quiet room, puzzling over equations and the mysteries of the universe, or playing violin, which helped him access a greater wisdom.

If he had always been out shopping and jamming to tunes—or reading other people's *updates* all day long, how could he have come up with the Theory of Relativity and become legendary?

Listening to Intuition

There are many different ways to listen more closely to your inner voice:

Journaling. When you sit down with blank paper, write your stream-of-consciousness thoughts like you are writing to God or your most beloved, caring friend. Get in touch with your feelings, your ideas, and your own solutions. Maybe something jumps onto the page that you didn't even know was in your mind. An answer may just pop into existence and surprise you. If you want to try something different from regular journal writing, you can try writing "morning pages," which Julia Cameron recommends in her book, *The Artist's Way*. She prescribes three stream-of-consciousness pages every morning to clear one's mind and access deeper guidance.

Another option is a process called "automatic writing," which means putting pen to paper and bypassing the conscious mind, allowing wisdom to come through. The idea is to get into a state of deep relaxation and then write without stopping, which allows your intuition to provide helpful information and encouragement.

It can take some practice to distinguish your intuitive voice from your ego or your own voice, but once you get the hang of it, you just may be surprised and delighted at what you can learn about yourself!

Meditating. Meditation can be as simple as sitting in a quiet place and breathing in and out for five minutes. Just notice your belly or chest expanding and contracting, or the air going in and out of your nostrils. There are so many ways to meditate, and you can find more classes, books, or apps than you could ever try. Just pick a way, and maybe down the road you can try another way.

If you practice it regularly, any meditation technique should help to clear your mind and put you more in touch with that quiet voice within. But don't feel too pressured or get discouraged. If you can only handle one minute of meditation, do one minute! You can even do "movement meditation," which is basically walking mindfully, or you can be mindful and tuned in while doing something you typically think of as boring, like washing dishes.

In his book *Getting in the Gap*, Dr. Wayne W. Dyer points out that the word "silent" has the same letters as the word "listen." He observes that this may not be a coincidence, because, "When you listen, you'll feel the silence. When you're silent, you'll hear at a new level of listening." He explains that silence creates a "gap" between this world and another realm, where guidance resides.

Also, this may surprise you, but meditation is helpful in a practical way (beyond just helping with intuition). Studies show that meditation activates the brain's frontal lobe, which is the area responsible for problem-solving, planning, and conscience. And who doesn't want to be a better problem-solver?

Meditation also activates the uppermost part of the limbic system, which generates feelings of empathy and compassion. So, meditating helps you be your best self by activating the most important parts of your brain! It turns out, it's not "unproductive" or wasting your time at all. I guess silencing your phone and detaching from all screens for a while isn't such a bad idea. Who knew?

Getting Balanced. Sometimes if we're too overworked, frazzled, stressed, sick, or not physically at our best, we can't access our intuition as easily. At those times, our intuition is like the sun that's temporarily hidden behind clouds. Then we need to come into better mental, emotional, and physical balance, which allows our intuition to shine brighter.

That's why it's helpful to engage in some sort of practice that helps you cultivate a clear and balanced mind. Maybe it's yoga, chanting, prayer, attending church, or doing Tai Chi or a martial art. Other helpful activities are exercise, ridding your body of environmental toxins using green powders and drinks (like wheat grass, spirulina, or chlorella) with a parent's supervision, and ensuring you get enough sleep. Make sure you're eating enough and that your meals give you lasting energy, which can mean balancing protein, carbs, and fats. Limit sugar and eat nutritious foods that help you feel balanced and more in tune with yourself and the flow of the Universe.

Praying. Ask for guidance from a Source greater than yourself. Say (silently, or out loud): "Please show me the right moves for the highest good of everyone involved." Or simply, "Please guide me in this situation." Then surrender all your brain's problem-solving efforts and give the issue over to the Universe, with much gratitude that "Thy will is done in the perfect way."

Watching and waiting. After asking with complete sincerity and letting the issue go, be watchful for any "hints" or "clues" that may come your way that are intuitive answers to your question. You might end up seeing something on TV or in a book that feels like "Hey—that's the answer!" Or a friend says something to you, and you think, "YESSSS!" Somehow you just "know" that you were given an answer.

Noticing your dreams. Sometimes, the Universe sends us messages in our dreams that answer a question or direct us about our next steps. Dreams can either be symbolic (like a puzzle to solve) or literal (like a psychic message from beyond).

It takes some experience to learn how to interpret dreams, but a good way to look at them is that every single thing in the dream represents a part of yourself. This is called the gestalt method. For instance, if you dream about a squashed cat, you're the squashed cat, and you probably need to deal with what's squishing you—or you might be squishing yourself! Your gut feeling is often the best guide as to what the dream is telling you. Special intuitive dreams often feel more "real" than usual. There's a reading list at the back of this book that includes a good book about dreams.

Once you receive your intuitive answer from any of these practices, you can say, "Hey, thanks, Universe! You're a real pal!"

The Time to Receive Guidance

Before asking for intuitive guidance, it's helpful to become relaxed. It's also important to create the intention to receive the most pure and positive guidance in the Universe. A prayer or affirmation can be used to prepare your mind to receive. It's also a good idea to avoid caffeine, sugar, medications, and alcohol before you ask for guidance, which allows you to be more centered and ready for accurate wisdom to arrive. Any authentic guidance you receive should seem friendly, encouraging, gentle, and positive, and it wouldn't tell you to do anything destructive or harmful.

Try this: Find a quiet place, get still, breathe, and relax, totally letting your mind and concerns recede from your awareness. Inhale white-light cleansing breaths, and exhale stress or tension. Intuitive teacher

Sherrie Dillard instructs, "Imagine a bubble of high-vibration white light completely surrounding you." Then ask a question that's on your mind, or just be completely open, asking, "What do I need to know right now?"

If you think you are getting a message, take note of it. Meditation teacher Eckhart Tolle explains that one way to identify your intuitive voice is when your decision or insight carries a "quiet strength behind your feeling" and "a peaceful quality to it."

Another sign that it is real intuitive guidance is that usually the guidance will contain short phrases or a single word instead of being chatty. In general, the source of guidance likes to be calm, direct, brief, and unemotional.

The Intuitive Body

A simple way to start receiving intuitive information is through body-based exercises. The solar plexus, or "gut" area, is often considered a primary place where intuitive feelings can be felt. However, others may feel their intuitions primarily in their heart area. To test which way works best for you, it's helpful to become quiet and ask your heart questions, as if you're talking to a friend, and see what answers emerge.

Alternatively, try this exercise: Lie down or sit in a comfortable position and become still and quiet. Let your tension go. Now, try making a statement such as *"I want to join that group,"* and see if it *feels true* inside of your body. Sense around. Do you feel anything? Warm tingles? Total *blah* blankness?

Or maybe the opposite statement—*"I don't want to join that group"*—feels truer. Does that make you feel the inner warmth that points to your personal truth? You can also use a comparison statement to check the truth of something. Lie down and notice how your body feels. Now say *"My name is Willow"* (using your own name, of course—or you can use something else that you know is indisputably true) and see how that feels in your body, right there in your solar plexus or "gut" area. Does it seem expansive, warm, good?

Great. Then say, *"My name is Pickles"* (or another name that's definitely not yours) and see how *that* feels. Cold, constricted, empty? Great. So then, when you're sorting out what's true, you want to feel in your body the same sense of "yes" or the calm-warm-bright-open-peaceful sense of truth that you felt in your body when you said your truth-testing statement. It is a good idea to start a body-based intuitive session with this truth-testing process.

Heeding Our Body's Signals

Body-image expert Virgie Tovar shares, "If we pay attention, our bodies are constantly sending us messages, letting us know what we like and don't like." For instance, Tovar says, when she is excited about something, "I open my eyes a little more, I smile, my toes and fingers wiggle a little bit, and I feel like the energy of my body is moving up through me—from my belly to my head."

Conversely, "When I'm not into something, I find that my eyes narrow a little bit, my body slumps a little, and I feel like the energy in my body is moving downward—from my head to my belly," she notes. If she *really* doesn't like something, "My stomach will drop a little, like I'm on a roller coaster."

Those are Tovar's examples, but you'll surely find many other ways of detecting what your wise, super-connected inner self really thinks. For instance, you've probably noticed the relief you sometimes feel after making a decision, such as declining an invitation or opportunity, or when something gets canceled. Even if that decision may be a bummer for others, you know by your feeling of lightness that it was right for you. Or, if you're disappointed something is canceled, that tells you that you really wanted it!

After meditating regularly, you may notice that you're in a good "zone," and suddenly you see or hear something that practically jumps out and says, "Notice me!" It could be a poster about an event, or a class listing, or a book, or even a phrase in a book you pick up. It could also be a person. Pay attention and consider those clues. You may want to let them sit for a wee bit before jumping in!

Some people find this guidance comes to them when they are in "the zone," which can happen during meditation or deep breathing but also while showering, biking, running, doing yoga, cooking, gardening, writing, painting, playing an instrument (like Einstein), while listening to certain music, while chanting, during prayer, while hanging out at a spiritual center of some kind, or while deeply connecting with another.

Your Unique Intuitive Code

Over time, you'll notice more feelings of being guided. You can experiment with how things turn out when you follow a hunch that something is right or ignore a feeling that something is wrong. Eventually, you will develop your own unique intuitive code. Your way of knowing things will be different from another person's.

For example, maybe you know something is the wrong move because you get a stomachache when you think about doing it. Or maybe you always get clumsy when you are trying to do too much. Perhaps you feel like you hear "No" inside your head ever so faintly when you "innocently" take something that isn't yours. Or maybe, when you stand on your head, you suddenly know the answer to your problems, because you speak the "Upside Down World" language fluently! Or maybe you're just a little different, and that's cool too!

Maybe you feel unexpectedly light and bright after you spend time with a certain person, or when you play checkers, or softball, or make a bracelet. Follow those things—you never know where they may lead.

The quote from famous mythology expert Joseph Campbell explains it well: "Follow your bliss and the universe will open doors where there were only walls."

This is because your "bliss" is blessed by the Universe.

Following your intuition is as much about finding those experiences that uplift and support your growing sense of bliss, purpose, and happiness as it is about avoiding those wrong turns and dead ends. Explains Judith Orloff, MD, bestselling author, and expert on intuition: "A master at reading vibes, intuition is constantly tallying what gives you positive energy; what dissipates it."

By following your intuition, you never need to be limited by circumstances—not ultimately—because there is always a part of yourself that is urging you on toward your greatness and happiness. This quiet voice is an ally in creating a better future.

There is comfort in knowing that an inner part of you (or the Universe) is always there for you. And that you can call upon this wise source of inspiration, knowledge, and guidance anytime!

"I think silence is one of the greatest gifts that we have."

—FRED ROGERS

EXPLORATIONS

Automatic Writing (or Inner Listening)

Find a quiet, comfortable place and sit with a pen and paper ready.

At the top of the paper, write down a question or issue you'd like guidance about. Phrase the question or issue as clearly as possible.

Close your eyes and take several deep breaths.

Ask your inner voice the question you wrote on the paper. It may take a few moments until you feel ready, but when you do, open your eyes and start writing whatever comes to you. It doesn't matter whether it makes sense or not. Keep writing until your hand feels like it won't move any longer, not reading what you have written as you go.

Now read over what you've written. You may be quite surprised at what wisdom has come out. Even a single word or phrase may be the key to your answer.

("Inner Listening" exercise, used by permission of Marci Shimoff.)

> "The weak can never forgive. Forgiveness is an attribute of the strong."
>
> —MAHATMA GANDHI

CHAPTER FOURTEEN

Opening Your Heart to Forgiveness

EVERYONE KNOWS that you're supposed to forgive. It's in the Bible, right? "Forgive them, for they know not what they do." It's kind of a no-brainer, and we get the message pretty early. Our parents start making us apologize when we are two years old and can barely say anything besides "More milk!" and "Me want ball!"

As we grow up, sooner or later, we hurt someone's feelings or make a mistake and try to make up, since generally it isn't all that much fun when people glare at us and curse under their breath as they go by. But you know what? The art of forgiveness—like, true forgiveness from the heart—is actually a really hard thing to do correctly. It's more than just saying "I forgive you." And doing it well is super important for our health and happiness.

Besides, we definitely want to be forgiven by others, right? I mean, which one of us hasn't done something really idiotic and wished we had magical "do-over" powers? We can act out of character; we can misperceive things because of our momentary emotions; we might lash out, say something really weird, or clam up and say nothing when people expect us to talk. So, hopefully people understand and forgive our imperfections.

But although we want forgiveness from others, sometimes it almost feels more right to hold a grudge against other people. Sometimes people make us so mad, so hurt, that we crinkle up our noses, turn our backs, and decide to ghost them. Our friends can reinforce these feelings and actions: *"She did what? No way!!"*

Sometimes, we are even still mad about something that happened months or years ago. We may think, *Gee, I sure wish that person would act better so I could forgive them. Why can't they be more thoughtful, more kind and considerate, and less mean, selfish, and totally rude?*

Why do some people act so bad, and what can we do about it? Do you ever wonder?

Of course. We all do!

But there's a simple and freeing answer: We forgive.

"Um, excuse me? Forgive mean people?" you may be asking.

Yes. Especially the mean people.

Here is the deal: Forgiveness is probably—almost certainly—one of the most important life skills you will ever have. You will achieve more inner peace by forgiving people than by meditating near a little stream in the mountains for a month. (Though, come to think of it, that would probably help too!)

You can have lots of friends, make the cheer team, attend prom with the hottie of the school, get elected class president, and be accepted to your dream school—later, have a good job, find the love of your life, and make lots of money—but without knowing how to really forgive others, you will keep getting stuck in these pockets of unhappiness.

Why Forgiveness Matters

Although most people do forgive, it is usually conditional. People often think it is enough to only forgive certain people who haven't done anything too bad or who they have to live with—*as long as* they stop doing those annoying things, or do them less often, or just, maybe, relocate somewhere else. But they cast the other, really heinous "villains" out of their hearts forever.

Unfortunately, that kind of forgiveness doesn't really get us very far. The problem is, people continue to do things that annoy or hurt us, and some of these people are never going to change. Not only will they not apologize—they will never even consider their behavior to be wrong!

So, our scorecards, judgments, and negative feelings keep weighing us down, never to be done away with, as we keep reliving the hurt feelings.

It may seem like forgiving people is the same as being a pushover, but it isn't being a pushover; it's being smart! In the words of Lewis B. Smedes, a theologian and ethicist, "To forgive is to set a prisoner free and discover that the prisoner was you."

When we don't forgive, we are the ones who actually suffer. In fact, every time we judge people, we feel worse inside on some level. We are trying to feel better by judging and resenting people—to get a little lift to our self-worth—but it doesn't work (or not for more than a nanosecond).

In the words of Nelson Mandela, who endured wrongful imprisonment for his efforts to work toward racial equality, "Resentment is like drinking poison and then hoping it will kill your enemies."

And that is partly because we live in an interconnected field of energy. What we put out and project onto others really affects *us* just as much. When we, instead, think positive, loving thoughts about others, our bodies, minds, and spirits feel better. Studies even show that forgiveness leads to better health.

Forgiveness is a way of *feeling inside*—an inner state—where it's almost unnatural to assign blame, resent others, or keep score. We are harmonious inside, trusting in life and love.

That doesn't mean we accept bad behavior and never stand up for ourselves. We still advocate for and take care of ourselves, which sometimes means removing ourselves from certain relationships and situations. We feel our feelings and honor ourselves. And then, we (yeah, you guessed it) forgive.

The Reality of the Golden Rule

In her book, *Trust Your Vibes*, Sonia Choquette counsels us, "Remember that you're intimately connected to everyone else in the world, so when you attack another person, you attack yourself. Regardless of whether or not our ego understands this, it is nevertheless true."

Surprisingly, "The Golden Rule" we learned when we were young refers to an actual law of life. Treat others as you want to be treated yourself, because you are *automatically* giving yourself what you give others.

According to the great American mystic and teacher Neville Goddard, those beliefs and feelings we have about others can come back to us like returned mail. These "unaccepted gifts" from us to the person in question boomerang back to ourselves and impact our lives.

His advice? "Only accept such states as true of others that you would willingly accept as true of yourself, that you may constantly create heaven on earth."

Does this mean we should try not to gossip about others? Absolutely! It's a hard habit to break, but our own happiness is on the line.

Choquette explains, "Know that words set the stage for coming attractions, so if you hear gossip, disengage; if someone is being critical, be silent. Walking away from negative conversation not only keeps your vibration oscillating at a higher rate, but it also protects others from lowering their vibrations by removing their audience."

Sometimes it can be quite difficult to break a habit of gossip, but the more you continue to change the subject to focus upon the positive, the more you'll find that your conversations become increasingly uplifting and fun. You can even talk about yourself more and admit your own difficulties in the area that's being gossiped about, to remind people that everyone has flaws and it's okay to be vulnerable.

The more you take time to process your own sad or mad feelings and the more you tend to your own destiny, the less you'll even *want* to think poorly of others. According to Sadie Robertson in her book *Live*, "Many times, we try to bring others down when we are feeling bad about ourselves." When you feel like you're on an equal playing ground, when you feel more secure within your own life and know your own power, you will have an easier time keeping negative comments from crossing your lips.

The Roots of Bad Behavior

Why *are* people so mean, anyway? Basically, it's because of this fact: Being human equals being riddled with insecurities. Pretty much everyone has unresolved insecurities or hurt feelings from their past. Most people are walking around with unresolved problems that they never got over, even if those things happened when they were tiny babies and they don't remember.

Unfortunately, most people are totally unaware of the things deep inside of them that cause them to act unkindly. Another factor in people's behavior is that, as you've probably noticed, "group think" is very powerful, and people can be swayed by others to function like obedient mindless robots, acting out their lingering anger or pain on others.

Also, sometimes people find it easier to connect with others based on their negative emotions (that come from past hurts) rather than their positive aspects. In that sense, people are innocent and unaware of themselves, and these lost souls deserve forgiveness.

We free ourselves from bad feelings when we see other people and situations like this:

They are doing their best.

They would do better if they could.

They suffer (on some level, even unknown to them), and therefore they are hurtful.

They want to be loved, just like I do.

They are trying to get their needs met, like I

am—even if their way, *to me*, seems misguided or counterproductive.

The less love that is in a person's heart, the more they need forgiveness and compassion.

We are more alike than different. We all have the same basic desires and feelings.

I can't know all the influences and events that have made that person how they are.

I can't control other people; all I can control is my reactions to them and the way that I think about them and approach them. In the words of Esther Hicks, "You can't control what other people do, but you can control what you're flowing [or offering] to others."

When I judge, it hurts me as much as it hurts anyone else.

When we understand the root of people's behavior (or just know that there *is* a root of it—a problem they never solved or reconciled), we can relax and not judge them. You will notice, *Hey, I feel better when I let go of negative emotions and thoughts associated with them. I guess I am really freeing* myself!

Really, if you're judging anyone, you're not understanding them. And no matter how people act, *everyone* can use more understanding.

In his book *Letting Go*, scientist David R. Hawkins shares a forgiveness mantra: "They, too, were doing what they thought was best at the time. We don't have to blame them or ourselves anymore. We can give up the whole blame game as obsolete and ineffectual."

It seems a little strange to approach things that way, but it can be quite freeing.

Rejection Calls for Forgiveness Too

Have you ever been rejected? Or at least wondered if you were being rejected? Guess what? This is another great time to practice forgiveness. Even though you might feel like "Ouch, that stings!", remember that we are *all connected*, whether we are currently choosing to spend time together or not.

Nothing can cut you off from Universal Love. Also, remind yourself that everything is a projection. The other person sees things as *they* are, not as *we* are. Not only is there no objective reality—there is really no such thing as separation. So, anyone who rejects others is also rejecting aspects of themselves or wrestling with full self-acceptance.

People always criticize what they can't accept about themselves or what they couldn't accept *if it were to be true* about themselves—which means they're confused about how life works and their own unconditional value.

Perhaps in some situations in which we feel rejected, people are just making the best choices they can at this moment, for whatever reason. Later they may think back and say, "Boy, I really made the wrong choice! What was I thinking?"

Ask for the *right* relationships to come to you, not just any relationships. Ask for the friends or situations you're *meant* to have, even if they don't match up with your preconceived ideas about the perfect situations right now.

In the meantime, you can say to yourself: "Rejection is not real. Only love and oneness are real." And think about this quote from Wayne W. Dyer: "The people who receive the most approval are unconcerned about it." Maybe, with a little help from your sweet little inner self, you can just let it go.

The wisdom of oneness is encapsulated in this statement by Byron Katie, a spiritual teacher I mentioned previously: "I am everything that I have called other people; they were me all along." In the final analysis, your relationship with yourself (and your inner source) is the only real relationship. Author Larry Dossey puts it well when he says, "Have compassion for others, for in some sense they *are* you."

Neville Goddard writes, in *The Neville Reader*: "Because life molds the outer world to reflect the inner arrangement of our minds, there is no way of bringing about the outer perfection we seek other than by the transformation of ourselves."

This is the loving task in front of us.

A Forgiveness Practice

A regular practice you can do is to sit and think of a person who really gets to you (whether you feel rejected by them or they just irritate or bother you) and send them love and blessings. Wish them every good thing. See them happy and thriving.

You may even want to see them being magically healed from the things that caused them to be unkind in the first place and therefore being happy and loving, in all their Divine perfection. By doing this, you release all ire and genuinely wish that they thrive. By sending it to another, in some crazy way you also send it to yourself.

What if doing that seems just *a bit* unfair?

Sure, I get it. It might be hard to become a saintly, all-forgiving ball of sunshine until you have helped yourself to feel that same love and unconditional acceptance.

I mean, who is forgiving and loving *you*?

You are. Aren't you?

Hmmm.

Reflect for a second: Do you constantly "beat yourself up" mentally about ways you should be better? Do you feel badly about yourself for certain things? Do you feel like if only you could just be a little different, you could finally totally love yourself?

If so (and which one of us doesn't sometimes treat ourselves that way?), *you* deserve to be forgiven for your own perceived imperfections. You deserve to hear from *yourself* all the wonderful things about yourself—for one, that you are a loving, thoughtful human who's smart and cool enough to get this far in a book like this. And about a million other things.

"You are altogether irreplaceable in the Mind of God" is a statement that appears in the beloved book *A Course in Miracles*. The next sentence is, "Whenever you question your value, say: *God Himself is incomplete without me*." This goes back to *all* of us being a perfectly, purposefully created ball of oneness.

The book also says, "You did not establish your value and it needs no defense. Nothing can attack it nor prevail over it. It does not vary. It merely *is*." No. Matter. What.

Virgie Tovar, in her wonderful book *The Self-Love Revolution*, drops this truth bomb: "You were born already enough, you are currently enough, and you always will be enough."

Honoring Yourself

Forgiveness is important, but guess what? Honoring your emotions and feelings is important too. It's important to listen to your feelings—they are there for a reason. Sometimes you may need to take time to heal from hurtful situations by talking with a friend, a family member, or a therapist.

You may want to explore other healing modalities that can most effectively help you feel more whole and healthier on every level: mentally, emotionally, spiritually, and physically. Certain relationships can certainly make us feel like we are *not* whole and perfect—although we actually are. And we deserve to take the time to be with ourselves in a loving way to restore our sense of perfection.

Sometimes if we communicate to someone what bothers us, the person will change their behavior—or at least try to. But if they don't, it doesn't mean they don't care about us or they are "bad." It just means that is the best they can do at this time. (Remember, if they could do better, they would!)

And even though it can be so easy to slip into self-pity when someone seems unkind to us, remember this quote from the Dalai Lama: "It is very rare or almost impossible that an event can be negative from all points of view." There is another way to see it. Maybe this gives you the opportunity to be assertive, be unconditionally okay with yourself, develop your spirituality, or advocate for others who experience unkindness.

You may be learning and growing through these challenges, and you can find the lesson or gift in the situation. If some person or situation keeps getting under your skin and causing you unhappiness, it's okay (or even essential) to take a break. Find a way to have your own little "time-out" and gather yourself up. Boost yourself up, do things you love, find your purpose, and connect with your inner self. Even forgo social media or most electronic communication for a while. It's okay to take care of yourself!

Meditate, affirm your beauty, soak up love from the Universe. You are not conceited or vain for thinking and feeling you are blessed with beauty and love, because you surely are. You deserve it as much as anyone else does. There is a reason the Buddha is quoted as saying: "You can search the world for someone who deserves love more than yourself, and you will never find it."

Tell yourself every day: "I love you and am 100% there for you in this life, no matter what."

"All forgiveness is self-forgiveness."

—MICHAEL BERNARD BECKWITH

EXPLORATIONS

Lovingkindness Meditation

One way to wish yourself and others well is to use this prayer from the Buddhist tradition, called a lovingkindness meditation. Sit for a few minutes and send love, like waves going out from yourself to the object of your attention. Start with yourself.

>May I be safe.
>May I be happy.
>May I be healthy.
>May I live with ease.

Repeat this many times, until you really feel that you are taking in those wishes for yourself.

After doing this meditation for yourself in the way it's written, send them to another person: "May Denise be safe, happy, healthy, and live with ease."

Finally, you can extend it to your family, your country, and the whole planet Earth or the whole Universe. Any subject is fine—the benefits will radiate to the rest of us, so there's no way to do it wrong!

"When your mind joins
with the mind of the universe,
something is created."

—JAMES VAN PRAAGH

CHAPTER FIFTEEN

Making Positive Changes

WE ALL WANT TO FEEL excited about life. We want to wake up bursting with enthusiasm for what lies before us. We'd love to be bouncing off the walls with giddy energy and the type of happiness that's almost too big to contain. Although, admittedly, bouncing off of walls may not be recommended, how do we move into a happier state? One in which it feels like everything is flowing in the right direction?

How do we find ourselves in a reality where all is right in the world (at least mostly), and we feel confident that our future will bring us more good times?

This chapter will outline a formula for bringing ourselves closer to this state, as well as providing key, often-overlooked considerations on how to best attract into our lives the happy times we wish for. Some people call this type of activity "manifestation"—a way of intentionally creating desired circumstances. Manifesting is based on the law of attraction, which states that "like attracts like," the act of drawing closer to whatever resonates from within us.

Or, if we prefer, another way to refer to manifesting is "co-creation"—the purposeful arrangement of life circumstances in coordination with a higher source. But first, let's discuss what manifestation or co-creation isn't. It isn't about controlling every single thing, making others do what we want, or forcing certain outcomes to happen, regardless of whether they're best for everyone involved. Which, from our ego's perspective, of course, kind of puts a damper on things.

For instance, wanting your ex-boyfriend back is a natural feeling, but proper use of manifestation techniques wouldn't be to focus single-mindedly on bringing him back to you. Maybe he is with someone else right now for his own growth and expansion, and it wouldn't be ideal for him to stay with you. Maybe he is learning important lessons on his own.

Even more importantly, maybe there's someone more fitting for you just around the corner. In order to attract them to you, however, you need to grow and change a little on your own. We are not here to influence others' destinies in ways that only serve our own single-minded desires. Desires are wonderful—don't get me wrong—but we also need to consider the big picture. Ideally, we want to create our lives in concert with a greater source of wisdom and intend the best outcomes for everyone, because we are all one.

Another thing to keep in mind—and it's a hard one—is that we need to try not to be perfectionists. Often we want life to look "perfect." We think everything needs to go "right" for us, and we can get the idea that if things aren't happening according to our perfect vision, something has gone wrong and everything is a disaster.

While it's lovely when everything lines up just how we want it to, sometimes it doesn't.

Accepting Life

What actually happens, most of the time, is *life*. Some great things, and also unfair situations and disappointing circumstances. The truth is, things *don't* always go so-called "right" in life—and that's *okay*.

There are times when you're on top of the world—you're the teacher's favorite student, you have a fun best friend, and you're a key player on your sports team. You're having an exciting time just being you and doing your thing.

Other times, things go a little south. Your friend finds another friend, you feel out of place, you come down with a never-ending cold, you get a haircut that looks like you were attacked by vengeful birds. While those things may feel terrible, none of them are wrong. It's *all* part of the fabric of life . . .

>Ups and downs,
>Ins and outs,
>Being together and apart,
>Winning and losing,
>Happiness and sadness,
>Struggle and flow.

This can be hard to handle if we *think* life is supposed to always be just *right*. But if we know that life has many facets, many moods, and both "desirable" and "undesirable" events, then we can adjust our expectations and become more able to *love what is*.

This is the power of acceptance. Acceptance can create miracles, and it's an important part of a proper manifestation practice. Acceptance transforms your energy from dismal to open and allowing. This invites grace and blessings to start flowing into your life.

So, whatever is happening—no matter how unwanted, unappealing, and absolutely maddening—send it love and acceptance.

You can accept when you study the wrong things for a test and don't get the desired grade. Or when you eat too much pizza for four months straight (winter is hard!) and don't fit into any of your pants anymore. You can accept it when you break your nose playing soccer and now you can't smell anything and look like you have a bird beak.

No matter what, there's only one thing to do: You say to yourself, with gentleness, "This is my life now, and it's OK." Accept and love your life *even with those things present*. Flow with the ever-changing current in your life without judging it. Learn to settle into your own space and be accepting of everything around you and within you. Let go of resistance and welcome it all with kindness. It doesn't mean you have to be excited about it.

When we think, *This shouldn't be happening,* Byron Katie asks us to inquire, "Is that really true? Do I absolutely *know* that this is true?" In other words, can we be totally sure that an experience we are having is "wrong"? Or is it actually our *perspective* about this experience that is wrong? What can this experience teach us, or how can it help us? Maybe, just maybe, there is something good in it. Often it's not the circumstances that are truly the problem; it's the way we're responding to them. It may not seem like it, but the truth is that we always have a choice.

We have a choice to cultivate what's called "psychological flexibility," which means we can do mental gymnastics and stick the landing into a new reality. In this reality, what happened is not a crisis, but a learning opportunity. In this reality, we still have options. In this reality, it's a chance to show our resilience and even take the world by storm. But it's not that easy.

The Law of Nonresistance

If you're like most people, you may have a hard time accepting things as they are. When you're uncomfortable, you probably want things to be different—immediately. However, when we resist our current reality, it prevents us from manifesting a new great future.

This is because of a little-known law that exists alongside the law of attraction called "the law of nonresistance." This law is summed up by the expression: *What we resist, persists.*

Remember the "observer effect" in quantum

physics? We affect matter with our minds. As we observe things, we make things more real and solid. It's often said, "Where attention goes, energy flows." That focused energy turns into physical reality.

It follows then that when we keep thinking about how awful something is, we attach ourselves to it with the sticky glue of negativity. When we put too much energy into something, even in a negative way, it is magnetized to us. If we don't give a hoot about it or remain unfazed, it falls away or changes more easily and effortlessly.

Hale Dwoskin, a teacher of a releasing system called the Sedona Method, explains that "When we are focused on wanting to change a problem, our awareness of the problem causes it to persist." This is because our mind (or attention to something) is creative.

It sounds odd, and a little mind-blowing, but the Universe doesn't distinguish between "focusing because I want this" or "focusing because I *don't* want this." It just responds like, "Okay, I've got your order. Another serving is coming up!"

The law of nonresistance tells us that instead of complaining and ruminating, it's better to let go and accept. And try to, as they say, "keep calm and carry on." Sometimes a huge dose of love is what the situation is asking for. You can mentally send love to any situation you're resisting.

It can be a challenge to stop lamenting and mentally cursing your circumstances. But one idea is to say statements like these when unwanted situations arise: "I resist nothing, and I anticipate so much good that's planned for me" or "I bless and send love to this situation and know that only good things come my way." Soon enough, you'll find it to be true. And follow the advice of Lao Tzu in the *Tao Te Ching:* "Be content with what you have, rejoice in the way things are. When you realize there is nothing lacking, the whole world belongs to you."

Accepting life doesn't mean we should be totally passive and do nothing about seemingly negative events. We can simply try to observe events in our lives like the weather passing through. If we don't like standing in a rainstorm, we can move inside and wait until it passes. We don't have to stand there getting drenched. Also, acceptance doesn't mean denying your feelings. The law of attraction is not about pretending you're happy when you feel upset about things. If you are feeling sad or mad, it's best to allow those feelings.

Setting Your Intention

Even while loving—or at least accepting, to the best of your ability—your life right now, you can (and should) be intentional about what kind of life you'd like to have in the future. We are always in a state of co-creation, molding life anew. We create new circumstances as a result of what we're thinking, how we're feeling, and our "vibes." And, of course, by our actions—especially when those actions come from a place of being in a peaceful state of alignment with the Universe.

One of the strongest ways to set new realities in motion is to set an intention.

What would you like to create in your life? A great haircut, clearer skin, a date with someone interesting, the perfect volunteer position, a new pet lizard, a new coat that fits your sense of style, or a spot on the dance team? You can empower yourself to create it, starting with bringing an intention into your mind.

Setting an intention is a bit like putting out a prayer to the Universe. As you do this, you join up with the Universe as co-creator. When you put your intention for your life out there, you broadcast a strong signal into an always-responsive field of possibility.

This process is explained by spiritual teacher

Ernest Holmes: "Prayerful communion ascends to that place where unity has not yet become variety, where the unformed One is ready to take any specific shape. In this act of communion the individual becomes copartner with the Eternal and gives birth to time, space, and conditions."

As that passage shows, we are powerful and can reach deep into the underlying field of the Universe to manifest new situations in our lives.

Getting into Alignment

You've already made great progress in beginning to manifest your dreams, but your work isn't done yet. The next step is to come into *alignment* with that new reality you seek. What does this mean? It means that instead of just saying, "Go ahead, Universe, bring me everything on a silver platter; I'll be lying around in my bathrobe and slippers, awaiting your service!", you must play a part in helping the manifestation come to pass. And that doesn't mean you have to work hard or stress out. It means you must transform yourself in positive ways so that this new reality can't help but be magnetized to you.

How can you do that? You do it by beginning to live in this beautiful future in your mind, emotions, and energy field. It may seem strange, but you have to start to feel and live as though something has *already* happened to you in order to bring it to you. Contrary to what everyone has told you forever and ever, you can't wait for good things to happen in order to feel happy. You must start feeling happier *beforehand.*

Yes, you heard me right! Switch the order of business to *finding happiness first*—or at least contentment, peace, or upliftment of some kind—before the happy circumstances can arrive. When you elevate your mood, your vibe, and your mental outlook, you create the conditions for your intentions to manifest. Another way to say it, in the words of interfaith minister Jean Sweet, is that you must find "emotional agreement" with the desires of your heart.

You want to feel and live in an emotional state that exemplifies a sense of "prosperity" or "fun friendships" or "class president." When you're acting like those things are true, those things can land more easily in your life and remain in your life instead of fading away.

Become a great friend, a great partner, a famous musician, or a stellar athlete within your mental and emotional world. Strut around like it's really happened. Use your creative imagination to your advantage. Look in the mirror and say, "Hey you, you're pretty amazing! I see what you did!"

It's not always easy to become aligned in this way. Sometimes it requires letting go of a belief that we are unworthy or releasing old stuck emotions that keep us feeling downtrodden. It can require ridding ourselves of the unhealthy habits that lower our overall vibe. It may even mean we have to *ixnay* certain relationships that don't help us see ourselves as capable and beautiful.

That all may sound daunting to you. There is, however, an easy and gentle path forward to releasing those things. Some of those ways include disputing negative thoughts and consciously focusing on the positive. Other ways are practicing gratitude, saying affirmations, visualizing, and engaging in a variety of uplifting activities and pursuits.

Focusing on the Positive

One of the first ways to help ourselves become aligned with good conditions and release old unproductive habits is to simply focus on the positive. What you focus on expands. One of Florence Scovel Shinn's sayings is "You combine with what you notice." So the first question we should ask ourselves is: What are we noticing?

Try to see only the goodness around you, both currently existing and soon-to-be-existing. See perfection. See beauty, success, kindness, and blessings. Speak only of the positive (except when you just need to vent and let off steam). Look for the good things that happen each day and the ways you're already provided for without making much effort. Notice other people's successes, beauty, sweetness, and kindness. Allow yourself to be affected by the cute dogs, the sunset, and the funny video.

Some people make a point to give out "awards" to the best things they notice each day. Author and teacher Marci Shimoff prescribes an exercise called "The Daily Happiness Awards." In this exercise, you identify the "cutest dog," "most adorable child," "most beautiful shirt," "prettiest flower," and either just award them in your head or go ahead and share the compliment with that person. This aligns your mind to the positive and spreads positivity in the process.

Disputing Negative Thoughts

If you find that it's hard to believe you deserve good things because you're just not quite worthy or don't have what it takes to pull it off, there's a way to address that. Byron Katie offers "The Work" to help people dispute negative thoughts and beliefs. We've already talked about the full version of The Work at the end of Chapter 1, but the shortcut is to first notice what you're saying to yourself. This might be something like, "I'm not popular enough to be class president."

Then ask yourself: Is it true? Is it unquestionably true, or could it be that I am just buying into a belief that isn't productive and isn't the full reality? Then find one to three opposite statements that can be just as true or truer. For example, "I AM popular enough to be class president."

At first, your opposite statement may seem hard to believe, which is why you then provide three examples of how each opposite statement could be just as true:

I am popular enough…because it isn't always the most popular one who wins.

I am popular enough…because there are other criteria like how good your speech is or what your campaign is based on or simply being smart, which I am.

I am popular enough…because I might be considered somewhat popular by a few groups of people.

I am popular enough…because I also know other people who weren't well-known or admired until they became class officers.

As you reflect more about what's causing you stress, you may even find that there is another belief that's even deeper down in your mind, which is: "I just have to be class president."

Is it true? Do you really *have* to be president? Counter that with an opposite: "I don't have to be class president." You'll realize that you were holding onto an untrue idea. You may *want* to be president, but if you don't become class president, you will be fine. You can still be a leader, accomplish goals, and feel special in a variety of other ways. You surely don't *have* to be elected.

When you learn to question your thoughts in this way, life will feel so much better.

Saying Affirmations

Because words have the power to affect our states of being, we have to watch the words that we think and speak. Are they positive or negative? The energy of words affects our bodies, minds, emotions, and lives.

When we direct our words purposefully toward a desirable experience, they become what's known as "affirmations." Repeating positive statements over and over can be an effective way to create more internal alignment with the circumstances we want to manifest.

A good affirmation might be something like "I have peaceful, joyful relationships," or "I am so grateful for all the fun I'm having with my wonderful friend!" or "I am happy and grateful to experience _____ in my life."

Keep in mind that while affirmations can give us a boost of hope, the results may not be seen immediately. This can be frustrating. It can feel like we're shouting affirmations into the void for weeks or months on end and nothing happens. "What's the point?" you may ask yourself.

Try not to get discouraged. Affirmations won't bring instant results in every case, because there are so many factors at play. You're working with a co-creative force that knows more about what you need than you ever could.

Sometimes there is a timing issue, and you just have to be patient and trust that you're in the right place at the right time, living the best life you can. Life will bring you new circumstances when it's time.

Pointers for Using Affirmations

A few tips to keep in mind when using affirmations:

Use present tense. Many wise teachers say that

affirming the results you want—stating them like they are *already happening now*—sets those realities in motion. Instead of focusing on what you see in front of you, withdraw your focus and mentally and emotionally focus on a different, more desirable situation and tell yourself that *that* reality is more concrete to you than the one in front of you. "I am completely rocking this math class, working out problems easily and effortlessly."

Focus on the feeling. When you state those new realities, notice how it makes you feel to state them. When you say them, do you feel energized and reassured, or do you feel the aching absence of the thing? Esther Hicks instructs us on the importance of the *feeling* of the affirmation rather than the actual words: "Rather than saying, 'I want or need a new car,' say instead, 'I like the *feeling* of Well-Being that comes with the driving of a new car,'—because you can accomplish that feeling even before you drive the new car; and once the *feeling* is consistently within you, the new car, and many other things that match your feeling of security, will flow to you."

Revise when necessary. As Hicks points out, the main point of your affirmations is to make you feel good, hopeful, and encouraged. This brings you more into alignment with great circumstances. Therefore, you should be particular about which words truly work for you. Adopting others' ideas about affirmative statements may not work as well.

Sometimes the affirmations can seem too far-fetched, such as "I'm a millionaire celebrity!" If this statement inspires feelings of doubt, disbelief, or stress (after all, the paparazzi are a real bummer to deal with!), it's not the right affirmation. In this case, reword the statement to make it more believable and uplifting.

Often the right wording brings you one small step in the direction toward the new circumstance and alleviates your worries, inner resistance, or disbelief. These affirmations may start with "I allow myself…," "I am worthy of…," or "I give myself permission to…[feel, be, or have those things you desire]."

As you speak and believe differently and truly begin feeling as if the words are true, you'll find your world shifting as well.

Visualizing Outcomes

Another wonderful way to bring you into alignment with your intentions is to spend time visualizing the outcome you want. Albert Einstein is quoted as saying, "Imagination is everything. It's the preview of life's coming attractions."

Florence Scovel Shinn wrote, in her book *The Game of Life for Women (and How to Play It!)*, "The imagination has been called the 'scissors of the mind,' and it is ever cutting, cutting, day by day, the pictures a woman sees there, and sooner or later she meets her creations in the outer world."

Studies even confirm this. When we visualize something, not only do our bodies respond as if it's actually happening (like our stress hormones start surging from simply imagining danger), but in some cases, actual physical reality can be altered. Weightlifters have been shown to gain physical benefits, such as strength, simply from *imagining* certain exercises. Can you believe that?

To make the power of visualization work for you, take time out of your life to picture a desired situation happening. See a detailed scene that says to you, "This already happened, and life is wonderful."

It can be a good idea to visualize before bed and/or right after waking up, when you're caught somewhere between waking life and dream life. This is when you're in the "zone," "vortex," or "field," mingling with the Universe in a more potent way.

In your visualization, make sure you realize your good fortune and celebrate your victory. Share the news with the people in your life. Look into their eyes and see their excitement. Grab onto the letter you received with the good news—or grasp the laptop or phone and show it to someone standing near you—and feel this new reality with all five senses. Sense how light, warm, and pleasant your body feels as you take in this new reality.

Competitive athletes use visualization techniques to see themselves executing their event perfectly before they compete. Trainers teach them to do that.

Jack Nicklaus, a world-champion golfer, has said, "I never hit a shot, not even in practice, without having a very sharp in-focus picture of it in my head."

Two-time gold medalist Olympic snowboarder Jamie Anderson explains, "Anything you do is 90 percent mental."

In sports as in life, what happens in your mind is just as important as—or even more important than—what you've trained your body to do.

If much of our reality is created in our minds, and if there is no permanent or unchangeable reality outside of ourselves, then we can always choose to see things:

In a more positive light.

With hopeful expectations of change.

As a blossoming, transforming situation.

As what we want them to be.

As we start to see things differently, it provides the impetus for new realities to take shape. As we truly feel and experience these circumstances happening, we naturally and easily find ourselves stepping into them in our physical reality.

Saying Thank You

While you're busy imagining yourself with your life's dream accomplished, don't forget your manners. Our parents may have been onto something when they constantly told us to say, "Thank you." This is because a state of genuine thankfulness is irresistible to the Universe. (Our parents probably didn't know that, but we'll still give them the credit.)

A state of thankfulness magnetizes the good to us. As we say thanks, we are in a state of seeing, believing, welcoming, and trusting the goodness of life. We feel truly grateful for the things that we are calling into our lives, which courts them with the right type of *attractive* energy instead of the negative energy of *Waaaah, I don't have this yet.*

"Thank you for what?" you may ask, if things aren't going your way right now.

Well, it's a little bit of a mind trick. You're thanking the Universe for the future that's on its way. You're conjuring up thankfulness for the fact that (in your mind's eye) it has *already* happened.

So, after you are done picturing yourself as an amazing musician attracting huge crowds or an expert debater delivering seamless arguments, you need to literally thank the Universe for those amazing gifts. Proclaim, "I am so grateful for…" with the most sincerity you can muster. As you say thank you, you are really convinced that this is happening now; it's your new reality. Feel the warmth of gratitude in your heart and in your body.

There is a reason that the Bible says, "Rejoice always, pray continually, give thanks in all circumstances; for this is God's will for you…" This is how we are meant to function—in a state of gratitude and trust—for both the present circumstances and the incoming future.

Gratitude helps us get into alignment with what we want, because it lifts our vibration. In the words of Michael Sandler, *Inspire Nation* podcaster and author of *The Automatic Writing Experience*, "There's a vibration to the partner that you want, the million dollars that you want, the peace that you want. All of it has its own unique vibration."

He instructs us, "Your job is to get in vibration with what you desire, and it will be yours."

Not that the point is to be greedy or that we need millions of dollars! We should approach life as a learning experience in "The Earth School." As humble students of life, we can only guess at what we truly need to experience. So, while we're striving for new beginnings and blessings, we should always remember to say "please." Asking with graciousness and receiving with gratitude is important, not just toward those in our lives but toward the Universe as well.

As we endeavor to transform our lives, the Universe will be at the ready, helping everything to happen perfectly. Shinn gives us a powerful affirmation of thankfulness and positive expectation that we can use: "I give thanks that I now receive the righteous desires of my heart. Mountains are removed, valleys exalted, and every crooked place made straight." Thank you, thank you, thank you!

> "Reality is much more malleable than anyone supposes."
>
> —DEEPAK CHOPRA, MD

EXPLORATIONS

My Powerful Mantra

Write down a statement that affirms your most positive, hopeful truth. This statement should describe your goodness, worth, and abundant success. Claim your new reality, your incoming good fortune, and/or your strengths and attributes. Rewrite it until you love it. Once you're happy with this statement and it makes you feel good inside, consider keeping it where you can see it regularly. And if you want to do more than one, have at it!

My powerful self-affirming mantra(s):

"Would you rather tell the Divine what to do or accept gifts the Divine has in store for you?"

—JOE VITALE

CHAPTER SIXTEEN

Stepping Into Your Destiny

AS YOU START TO BE MORE in alignment with the Universe, you'll be able to step into the best version of your life that's out there just waiting for you. We talked in the last chapter about how to get into alignment, and in this chapter we'll talk about a few more ways to do that, plus how to harness the power of gratitude and surrender to access your highest destiny.

There are a variety of ways to uplift yourself into new realities and clear out any obstacles to attracting them. This can include anything that makes you feel better (if it's something healthy that's good in the long run as well). Yes, enjoyment and happiness can attract more good things from the Universe.

So, ask yourself: *What makes me feel happy?* Do you

love singing, dancing, or crafting? Make time for those things, because they make you more aligned with all the good stuff. Are you happiest when you hang out with certain types of people? Make time for those people—or find where they hang out and introduce yourself. Build your happy world.

Self-care is also something that can improve your outlook. Self-care activities can be as simple as letting yourself rest, getting adequate sleep, taking a long Epsom salts bath, or going for a leisurely walk. In fact, exercise is an excellent way to uplift your mood because it causes your body to produce endorphins, which makes you feel better.

Many more holistic therapies are aimed at helping you feel more peaceful and content, including meditation, yoga, acupuncture, massage, reiki, and many more. Any of those can help raise your vibration so that you're more ready to receive. And, of course, any way you can get into a state of oneness is a potent way to shift your energy into a state of receiving.

Often, to get into alignment, we need to release negative emotions and improve the way we talk to ourselves. With a therapist, we can address underlying emotional wounds. We can also work on identifying self-defeating beliefs through cognitive-behavioral therapy (CBT) and emotional freedom technique (EFT). There are many books and videos that can address this as well.

Gratitude: The Attractor Factor

In the last chapter, we spoke about the important step of saying thank you when actively manifesting, but gratitude deserves its own devoted section. That's because out of all the things you can do to co-create a better life, practicing gratitude day in and day out just might be the most important.

Those who study the law of attraction and those who study brain science have arrived at the same conclusion: Gratitude practices (and other heart-based practices such as the ones from HeartMath Institute you saw at the end of Chapter 12) are the key to a new brain, a happier body, and a transformed life. This is because when you practice it enough, gratitude changes your brain and how you're being in the world.

In the field of positive psychology, studies show that gratefulness practices increase happiness levels. Neuroscientists have discovered that regularly expressing gratitude rewires your brain in a positive way—especially if you really *feel it* and let those good feelings sink in for two or three breaths.

As we develop new neural pathways in our brains by repeated and sustained feelings of gratitude, we start to be in a more positive mood. Then we begin sending out improved signals to the Universe. Before we know it, our entire world changes in response to our new state of being.

According to quantum healer Joe Dispenza, gratitude is so important because it signals to the Universe that "something wonderful just happened." This is also true even if you're thinking about something from the past.

When we're in a state of "something wonderful just happened," then we are clearly ready and able (in the Universe's eyes) to receive wonderful things. We are showing that we know what receiving the good stuff is all about!

One simple and effective way to express gratitude is to keep a gratitude journal and add three things you're grateful for each night before bed. In fact, researchers have found that a gratitude journal is the number-one happiness lifter of all the happiness-raising techniques studied. If every night isn't realistic, once a week can be very effective.

If writing things down isn't your jam, you can

instead do silent prayers of thanks each night for all the blessings in your life. As another option, you could say your gratitude out loud to someone or make it a family dinner ritual everyone can benefit from.

Television mogul Oprah Winfrey has said, "What you focus on expands, and when you focus on the goodness in your life, you create more of it. Opportunities, relationships, even money flowed my way when I learned to be grateful no matter what happened in my life."

The Magic of Surrender

Now that you're more aligned, there's one more thing you must do if you want to manifest the good stuff. I must warn you though, it's going to sound counterintuitive: You have to surrender. *Surrender? After all that work to develop intentions, craft affirmations, and create gorgeous visualizations? Why?*

Surrendering is important because we are co-creators. We have a lot of power, but we're coordinating with an even greater power. We don't want to get into a tug-of-war. We want to cooperate. This means we must release our plans to the Universe. Surrendering is one of the least understood aspects of the law of attraction. It's not something most of us are very familiar with. In a general sense, surrender is thought of as a negative thing—as not taking charge enough or being defeated.

That's why surrendering is a scary thought to most of us. We've been taught that we have to buckle down and work hard to create the future we want to achieve. We've been taught that we have to power through and force circumstances into being. Only then will we get the As, the scholarships, the leadership positions, or the medals and trophies we covet. All the while, we are scanning for competition, muttering to ourselves "I probably won't get it," and redoubling our efforts.

But when we do this, we aren't really clearing the space for the Universe to deliver the goods. We are, instead, resisting the flow of life. We're not in a relaxed, open, trusting state. Yet a relaxed and open state is what we need to be in if we want to invite in new and different situations. In fact, an interesting research study has even shown that it works better to "wish lightly" for something to happen instead of intensely turning all our focus toward something.

As explained by Esther Hicks: "The releasing of resistance will bring you everything you want."

Florence Scovel Shinn proclaimed something

similar, advising us to try to relinquish our will: "A woman is admonished [by the Divine], 'My will be done, not thine,' and the curious thing is, a woman always gets just what she desires when she does relinquish personal will, thereby enabling Infinite Intelligence to work through her." In other words, when we release our will and invite a higher will, that's when the magic really happens.

Surrendering allows the Universe to bring us miracles in its own creative way. If we keep holding tight, thinking we have to "figure it out," we aren't truly letting go and accepting the help that we need. When we surrender, new beginnings come to us that are often better than we could have orchestrated ourselves—or even dreamed were possible.

In fact, the more loosely we hold something, the more the Universe steps in and delivers. Sedona Method teacher Hale Dwoskin has noticed that people actually manifest more when they surrender more. It kind of makes sense. Have you ever noticed that when you don't really care about something, it comes to you easily?

"We think we don't have what we want because we haven't wanted it enough. But the exact opposite is true," Dwoskin explains. "The more you let go of wanting, the more you feel like you have and the more you manifest in life."

Mic drop!

So, knowing everything is being handled perfectly by a power greater than yourself, you can breathe a sigh of relief and let go. You can put your own ideas and solutions aside. Soften your grasp on the situation and open yourself to a greater wisdom, trusting in life to bring you exactly what you need. Declare: "This or something even better, according to the Intended Plan for my life (or, 'according to the highest good of all')."

As you let go, you'll begin to claim what is rightfully yours: good experiences, happy accidents, fateful twists of luck, good fortune, abundant resources, unexpectedly pleasant situations, and much more that you never knew could be yours.

Shinn offers an affirmation to do upon waking: "Thy will be done this day! Today is a day of completion; I give thanks for this perfect day, miracle shall follow miracle and wonders shall never cease."

Take Inspired Action

Remember that even after surrendering, you are still an important player in this game. You still need to take action, putting one foot forward toward that goal, going in the right direction with your everyday actions while you picture the perfect result.

Of course, the best actions are those that are guided by our intuitive sense that's connected to the wisdom of the Universe. In the words of Esther Hicks: "Make very sure you're under the influence of Source before you follow any impulse."

Being under the influence of a higher power means not letting negative emotions, such as desperation or fear, drive our actions. Before we take action, we need to try to settle down inside and get in touch with greater wisdom.

We need to touch that sense of stillness. In the words of Frederick Chavalit Tsao, co-author of *Quantum Leadership*, "In order to connect with The Source, we need to still our mind. Only through stillness are we closer to the reality of the fundamental field, which is entirely still."

One way to ensure you're under the influence of the Source or Universe is described by quantum physicist Amit Goswami, PhD, who recommends a process called "DO BE DO BE DO." It sounds like a silly throwback song from the 1950s, but it's also a serious formula for making your dreams come true.

He recommends that you alternate back and forth between spending time in a "being" place of connecting with the Universe, then going out and "doing" what you need to do to bring things to fruition.

It's a good reminder, because we can sometimes get stuck in the doing (constantly working toward a goal, even when it's getting us nowhere) or the being (just sitting around visualizing dreamy scenarios all day long), but we need *both*! And, ideally, we want those "doings" to be connected to a deeper "knowing" about what's right.

The Divine Design

By now you're probably getting the picture that manifesting or co-creating isn't about forcing outcomes we want; it's about being open to what's best. But what *is* best? How are you supposed to know?

Is there some kind of a cosmic plan? We talked about destiny in Chapter 11, and we established that there probably is one.

You may wonder: *If there's a destiny, why do I have to do any of this at all?* The truth is that we have to balance destiny with creative action. Likely we all have a destiny. Yet, we also have free will—our freedom of choice (like Anita Moorjani talked about in an earlier chapter). We can exercise our free will to create the conditions of our lives, though there will always be a force beyond our control that is contributing to what happens.

Certain things (like graduating from high school or college) may happen regardless, but for other things to happen, it may require that we rally our manifesting powers. Life is a creative process, and we should be engaged participants. Yet we have to know when to surrender and let go.

Sometimes, to realize what's truly best in a situation, we must do a bit of detective work. We can see if we can sense or feel what the optimal goals are for our lives, and we can become more sensitive to receiving those insights. Florence Scovel Shinn, whom I mentioned many times before, was a big proponent of aligning with one's "divine design" for their lives. This design is a bit like a blueprint for a house or a story outline.

The idea of a divine design is that the Universe is handing you a basic outline for a story—a beautiful, triumphant story of a life fulfilled. In this outline, you've been provided with the characters, the setting, the basic plot, and the main events. Your job is to fill in the details of the story with your own creativity in ways that align well with the original outline.

To discover the outline we've been handed, Shinn recommended that we become still and receptive. In the stillness, we allow the Universe's perfectly planned future to show itself to us rather than trying to force a visualized picture of something we *think* we need.

In a passage from her collected works, *The Writings of Florence Scovel Shinn*, Shinn explains this approach: "Visioning is a spiritual process guided by intuition, or the superconscious [Universal] mind. The student should train his mind to receive these flashes of inspiration and work out the 'divine pictures' through definite leads. When a person can say, 'I desire only that which God desires for me,' his or her false desires fade from the consciousness, and a new set of blueprints is given him or her by the Master Architect, the God [or Universe] within."

To translate that, we want to let the influence of the ego (which Shinn calls "false desires") fade away. This allows the blueprint (the greater plan of the Universe) to reveal itself. This blueprint will reveal itself in inspirations and visions.

As you strive to accomplish your goals, know there's a Universe that's standing by, rooting you on and helping you every day. Know that the best, most amazing good fortune, custom made for you, is surely coming to you in the right timeline.

Say thank you, surrender, and trust that everything that happens is always perfect. Whether you call it good or call it bad, the events of your life are always moving you along toward your greatest and brightest destiny.

You're never alone—there's a whole interconnected Universe on your side. You've got this!

> "Things have no reality other than in consciousness. Therefore, get the consciousness first and the thing is compelled to appear."
>
> —NEVILLE GODDARD

EXPLORATIONS

My Ideal Day

In this exercise, you'll imagine your ideal life. Doing this exercise can feel like you're writing a letter to the Universe about what you want your life to be, and it's fun to imagine all the tantalizing details. Once it's written, you can trust that it is being taken care of (this ideal day—or something even better, of course).

This is a good exercise to do every few years—at least every five years—to make sure that your life is unfolding according to your deepest wishes and hopes. It will help you chart a big-picture course for your life. You might want to go back and read through this periodically to remind yourself of what you really want.

Write about your ideal day and what that includes, from the time you wake up in the morning to right before you fall asleep at night. Really dream big about what you would like your life to look like. Describe your activities and the feelings you experience during your day. Start with waking up in the morning and include every part of your day until you go to bed at night. What happens during the day? What surrounds you in your life? Use a separate piece of paper, if needed.

_____
_____
_____
_____
_____
_____
_____
_____
_____
_____
_____
_____
_____
_____
_____
_____
_____

Meditation for Manifestation

This potent manifestation meditation includes everything you need to properly co-create. It draws from the wisdom of many great teachers, including Joe Dispenza, Esther Hicks, and Florence Scovel Shinn, as well as manifestation processes from the Science of Mind spiritual tradition. You can do this daily or as often as possible to help you more easily co-create a beautiful future.

1. Sit or lie down in a relaxing position. Become mindful as you notice your breath going in and out of your nostrils or as you feel your chest or belly rising and falling. Do this for 30 seconds or more.

2. Listen to the sounds in the room (like the heater or air conditioner) or sounds outside of your room (like people talking or the noise of the television).

3. Notice your breath as it goes in and out while giving open and aware attention to the various sounds you hear. See if you feel calmer as you are present in this way.

4. Feel yourself blending with everything around you, just for this moment in time. Notice that there is no division between your body and the space surrounding it.

5. Acknowledge an awareness of something you would like to create in your future. See a vivid scene of something good happening in your life. Allow the picture to fill in with more details as you simply surrender to it. What do you see? Hear? Smell? Touch? Give yourself at least a few minutes to experience the scene.

6. Sense your feelings. When the picture is filled in as much as it can be for now, try to feel what the "you" in this situation is feeling like. Do you feel uplifted? Warm? Light? Excited and tingly? Try to locate those feelings in your body now. Hold those feelings if you can. Let them wash over you or fill you up.

7. Affirm this new reality with an affirmation or declarative statement. (e.g., "I am now a marine biologist.") Express thanks for this new reality coming into your life. Really feel the gratitude for it.

8. Then let it go, saying, "This, or something better, according to my highest good and the highest good of all."

When you feel complete, come back to the present moment. If you need to come back into your body more fully, do a grounding exercise like putting your feet on the ground and imagining cords, roots, or light rays connecting you from the bottoms of your feet or base of your spine to the center of Earth.

"When we try to pick out anything by itself, we find it hitched to everything else in the universe."

—JOHN MUIR

CHAPTER SEVENTEEN

Putting It All Together

Most likely, this book has been a real eye-opener, introducing you to many new ways of seeing and navigating your amazing life. You might still be trying to sort through all the ideas presented in the book, or you might be jumping right into using them. Regardless of what point you're at with these concepts, these are a few milestones you can expect to reach along the journey to a life aligned with oneness:

You're acknowledging your interconnectedness. First of all, you may be starting to see your life in a more interconnected way (hopefully!). Instead of feeling alone in your struggles, you may be realizing you can relax a little more and accept that you're supported and guided by the Universe.

You're changing your perspectives. You've now realized you can choose to view yourself and your life differently and that you deserve to have a sense of empowerment about your circumstances. The idea that you're stuck being a certain way? The belief that you're a victim of your environment? Those beliefs are fading as you've started questioning your thoughts and broadening your viewpoint. Plus, you're becoming less judgmental day by day, which helps everything in your life work better. You now know that, as an interconnected being, your thoughts are powerful. You're sculpting your life with your positive thoughts and intentions, and you now have specific exercises to help you do so.

You're excited to embrace your unique purpose. It may feel comforting knowing that there is a special purpose for your life and that your life journey will be partly about discovering that. Instead of thinking you have to go down paths that others have prescribed for you, you realize you have clues already inside of you pointing toward your purpose and destiny. As you trust this, you are looking for "flow" and noticing what the Universe is nudging you to do. This helps you feel reassured that all is on track and nothing is wrong. While you travel your unique path, you are spending as much time as you can doing things that truly light you up.

You're learning to tap into the Source of all. As you follow the book's exercises and begin to notice more instances of oneness, you're starting to tap into a sense of unity with everything. You may feel a warm, bright, or calm sense of merging with a greater Universe, and this has started to comfort you. What's more, you've begun to commune with the Universe to receive intuitions about your best choices. You may notice sudden realizations or "light bulb" moments, calm feelings of rightness, a sense of warmth within, or a written answer suddenly appearing on a piece of paper or computer screen through automatic writing. You're acting on those insights and life has become more interesting and fulfilling.

You're becoming empowered to change your life. You're starting to visualize new situations in life and set intentions for what you'd like to co-create. While you might not always be sure whether or not what you desire is going to happen, you know it's equally important to be grateful for what's here now. Sometimes it's just about having faith that everything you need is truly available if you're aligned with the Universe and vibing high.

You're following a new road map. Finally, you're ready and willing to chart a new course for your life based on this book. You're using the book when you need a pick-me-up or a counselor to guide you along on your path to greatness. This road map is helping you to become more and more of the real you and to live a life that you truly want. In a world that seems to lead you down superficial, unfulfilling paths, this is quite an accomplishment. With this new approach to life, you're not only going to find the perfect path for yourself, but you're going to make this world better. I'll see you on the trail!

"When you get to a place where you understand that love and belonging, your worthiness, is a birthright and not something you have to earn, anything is possible."

—BRENÉ BROWN

> "Humankind has not woven the web of life. We are but one thread within it. Whatever we do to the web, we do to ourselves. All things are bound together. All things connect."
>
> —CHIEF SEATTLE

Onward

There will come a time, even in the Western world, when it will be considered normal to acknowledge a greater source of wisdom. It will become commonplace to take a moment to meditate and to consult with our intuitive voice. This new world simply must come to pass, because otherwise we will not be able to become the world we need to be in order to survive and to flourish.

In this new world, families will honor this need to go within. Friends will ask each other, "Did you go within and check whether that's right for you?" Your bestie will say, "If you want that to happen, you need to spend time connecting with a Divine Source/Spirit/Universe." It will become, finally, an intuitive and interconnected world rather than a rational, logical, materialistic world, which has brought all of us and the entire planet so much trouble.

You can be on the cutting edge of this new world, demonstrating to others a new way to live as oneness. You can take time to sit with yourself and become aware of your interconnectedness with everything. You can start to appreciate yourself and accept your uniqueness. You can notice what you feel called to do. You will gravitate to the things that really resonate with the deepest part of you and make you feel you are home. You can be a beacon of unconditional love and compassion, both for yourself and for everyone you meet.

In closing, I want to share the following passage with you that contains the words received by Suzanne Giesemann, a professional intuitive. I hope that this will encourage you as you go forward in creating your own amazing life:

"You are being led moment by moment. Are you listening? Perhaps you are charging this way and that, unable to relax for there is a nagging feeling that you are not enough, not good enough, not worthy enough, not successful enough. Allow us to narrow it down: Most humans feel they are not loved enough, and nothing could be farther from the truth.

"This is the guidance that is being sent to you moment by moment, fed through the heart, if only you would take down the barriers that went up brick by brick as fellow hurting humans hurt you. You are enough exactly as you are at your very core. You are Love in Full Expression. Hold this Truth in your heart and bring it into full awareness. Go forth confidently, unscathed by those around you. You are so very loved. You would drop to your knees if you could feel the full force of it."

> "Even if I knew that tomorrow
> the world would go to pieces,
> I would still plant my apple tree."
>
> —MARTIN LUTHER

FURTHER READING AND LISTENING

50 Ideas You Really Need to Know: Quantum Physics
by Joanne Baker

Ask and It Is Given: Learning to Manifest Your Desires
by Esther and Jerry Hicks

Angel Intuition: A Psychic's Guide to the Language of Angels
by Tanya Carroll Richardson

The Artist's Way: A Spiritual Path to Higher Creativity
by Julia Cameron

The Automatic Writing Experience: How to Turn Your Journaling Into Channeling to Get Unstuck, Find Direction, and Live Your Greatest Life by Michael Sandler

Be True to Yourself: A Daily Guide for Teenage Girls
by Amanda Ford

The Bond: How to Fix Your Falling-Down World
by Lynne McTaggart

Breaking the Habit of Being Yourself: How to Lose Your Mind and Create a New One by Dr. Joe Dispenza

The Field: The Quest for the Secret Force of the Universe
by Lynne McTaggart

The Game of Life for Women(and How to Play It!)
by Florence Scovel Shinn

Getting in the Gap: Making Conscious Contact with God through Meditation by Dr. Wayne W. Dyer

Getting into the Vortex by Esther and Jerry Hicks (book and audio recordings)

Grounding: Coming Home to Your Self by Nell Arnaud

Happy for No Reason: 7 Steps to Being Happy from the Inside Out by Marci Shimoff

Hardwiring Happiness: The New Brain Science of Contentment, Calm, and Confidence by Rick Hanson, PhD

Ho'oponopono: Your Path to True Forgiveness by Dr. Matt James

The How of Happiness: A New Approach to Getting the Life You Want by Sonja Lyubomirsky

The Invisible String by Patrice Karst

Living in the Light: Follow Your Inner Guidance to Create a New Life and a New World by Shakti Gawain

Living Your Dreams: Using Sleep to Solve Problems and Enrich Your Life by Gayle Delaney, PhD

The Neville Reader by Neville Goddard

The Physics of God: How the Deepest Theories of Science Explain Religion and How the Deepest Truths of Religion Explain Science by Joseph Selbie

Quantum Physics (Idiot's Guides) by Marc Humphrey, PhD, Paul V. Pancella, Phd, Nora Berrah, Phd

The Secret by Rhonda Byrne

The Sedona Method: Your Key to Lasting Happiness, Success, Peace, and Emotional Well-being by Hale Dwoskin (book and free YouTube movie)

The Self-Love Revolution: Radical Body Positivity for Girls of Color by Virgie Tovar, MA

Trust Your Vibes: Live an Extraordinary Life by Using Your Intuitive Intelligence by Sonia Choquette

The Untethered Soul: The Journey Beyond Yourself by Michael A. Singer

Wolf's Message by Suzanne Giesemann

The Writings of Florence Scovel Shinn by Florence Scovel Shinn

You Are Psychic: Develop Your Natural Intuition Through Your Psychic Type by Sherrie Dillard

www.ingramcontent.com/pod-product-compliance
Lightning Source LLC
Jackson TN
JSHW021644120825
89261JS00003BA/15